.od

D1431901

EDWARD C. MIGDALSKI as a boy developed an enthusiasm for fishing that led him to study fishery science at Cornell and at Yale. Now at Yale, he is Ichthyologist in the Bingham Oceanographic Laboratory; Chief Preparator of Fishes, Peabody Museum; Director, Outdoor Recreation and Minor Sports, Yale Athletic Association; and Fishing Coach. He is also Director of the Intercollegiate Game Fish Seminar and Fishing Match held annually in Nova Scotia, and Chief Judge, United States Atlantic Tuna Tournament. Other books by Mr. Migdalski published by The Ronald Press Company are *Boy's Book of Fishes, Angler's Guide to the Salt Water Game Fishes—Atlantic and Pacific,* and *Angler's Guide to the Fresh Water Sport Fishes of North America.*

HOW TO MAKE
FISH MOUNTS
AND
OTHER FISH TROPHIES

EDWARD C. MIGDALSKI

BINGHAM OCEANOGRAPHIC LABORATORY
AND PEABODY MUSEUM OF NATURAL HISTORY
YALE UNIVERSITY

THE RONALD PRESS COMPANY · NEW YORK

Library of Congress Catalog Card Number: 60–6156

To
My Son
Tom

Preface

Every angler with more than just a passing interest in fishing can recall the occasion when he wished that his catch could be preserved. The prize was perhaps an unusually large example of his favorite game fish. Or it may have been an unusually beautiful specimen—well colored or well proporitoned—which he pictured as an attractive piece of décor in office or home. Perhaps the trophy was of sentimental value in recalling a "trip of a lifetime." But in the end, the thought was sadly dismissed, perhaps with an audible sigh, "Too much trouble" or "Too much money" and usually, "How would you go about it, anyway?" This book will show the average angler how he can go about it cheaply and easily—and have a lot of fun at the same time.

Many fishermen must think twice before carting their fish to a taxidermist, for good craftsmanship is expensive. Even if he can afford it without undue strain on his pocketbook, the angler may be several days away from civilization and consequently will give up a fine trophy because he believes it is extremely difficult or greatly inconvenient to preserve the fish long enough to reach a taxidermist. Then there is the man who would feel genuine satisfaction from admiring his catch on the wall but who shudders just to think of his wife at the front door, as he carries in the mounted fish, saying, "You are not coming into *this* house with *that* monstrosity." And many young boys would derive great value from making a collection of fishes, but they are discouraged from attempting it because of the common thought that the project is too complicated.

Part of my life's work at the Bingham Oceanographic Laboratory and Peabody Museum at Yale University takes in the planning of exhibits for a fish hall, including field collecting and laboratory preparation. Therefore, I am in a position to witness the great interest shown in fish taxidermy and collecting by anglers of all types and ages—boy scouts, camp counselors, students, teachers, commercial taxidermists, and museum workers from around the United States and different parts of the world. During the course of a year, I receive many enthusiastic inquiries in person, by mail, or by phone.

A single attitude is common to all—the prevailing thought that preserving and mounting fish is very difficult. It is not. That is why I have been induced to write this book. Any angler who has the ability to cast a line or wind a reel can preserve his prize catch—easily and at negligible cost. No outstanding scientific or artistic ability is required to produce a pleasing, decorative trophy by one of the many methods described on the following pages—information that is not easily obtainable elsewhere. The fisherman who is miles away from home will find that he can care for his prize fish by employing a method that requires little time and only a small space in his car, with no ice or refrigeration needed! If the angler's wife disapproves of monstrosities on the home walls, her attitude toward fish trophies can be changed dramatically by simply introducing her to a clean-cut plastic mount, without the ugly backboard present on most commercially mounted fish—a trophy with little weight that can be hung easily anywhere to fit in with the house plan or decorations. For those who want even simpler methods, I suggest an outline of the prize catch in wood or mounted on art board. Or the head, tail, or bill of the fish can be dried and preserved. And finally there is always the photograph, where a few practical hints can make all the difference between a stiff, unnatural picture and a pleasing record of a memorable event.

Boys who have an interest in the out-of-doors are always attempting to form collections, and most of them try a hand at some sort of taxidermy. Parents whose children indicate such interest are fortunate, and they should encourage their offspring whenever possible. I have included methods of working with fishes that can fit into the specific interests and capabilities of any age group of young boys. Twenty summers of experience have brought home to me the importance of nature study and museums in summer camps. Annually, at the approach of spring, I receive inquiries from school and college students, and others having summer jobs at boys' camps, who are interested in establishing a program concerning fish. This has led me to include a complete section of instructions on collecting, preserving, and displaying a fish collection intelligently at summer camps and other holiday resorts—inland or along the seashore. An organized activity of this type can be of inestimable value to any summer camp.

Last, but not least, because I am also a professional museum man, I am in constant touch with the latest development in methods of preparation. Through trial and error, mostly in the field, I have developed methods which perhaps are not generally known to other scientists because they have never been published. Chapter 10, Fishes in Museums of Natural History, should be of value to scientists, commercial taxidermists, and anglers who are interested in advanced techniques.

I strongly recommend that before attempting any method included in this volume, the angler first read the entire book.

EDWARD C. MIGDALSKI

New Haven, Connecticut
January, 1960

Contents

CHAPTER   PAGE

1   FIELD CARE OF FISHES   3

Color photos and notes, 3 · Protecting the specimen, 4 ·
Preventing spoilage, 6

2   PLASTER MOLDS   14

Molds and casts, 14 · Mixing the plaster, 15 · Molding a
fish, 15 · Molding in the field, 31 · Molding at home, 35

3   CASTS   38

Preparing the Mold for Casting, 38 · Show side of mold,
41 · Rear half of mold, 41 · *Casts in Plaster*, 45 · *Casts
in Wax*, 48 · Wax casts—half mold, 49 · Wax casts—full
mold, 54 · Fins, 55 · *Casts in Compound*, 55 · *Casts in
Plastics or Resins*, 59 · Applying plastic, 59 · Strength-
ening the cast, 66 · Securing the halves, 69 · Removing
cast from mold, 70 · Cleaning and finishing the cast, 70 ·
Fins, 74 · Mouth, 78 · Eye, 78 · Bills or spears, 78

4   SKINNING AND SKIN MOUNTS   81

Skinning the Fish, 81 · Preserving the skin, 88 · *Skin
Mounts*, 90 · Mounted skins, 90 · Excelsior body, 91 ·
Wood mannequin, 91 · Skin mounts—half mold, 93 ·
Skin mounts—full mold, 101

CHAPTER   PAGE

5   PAINTING THE MOUNT   104
    Preparing the surface, 104 · Simple painting, 112 ·
    Painting with oils and brush, 112 · Painting with lacquer
    and airbrush, 113 · Painting the glass eye, 115

6   OUTLINES AND SILHOUETTES   116
    Pen and ink outlines, 116 · Art board silhouettes, 118 ·
    Color combinations, 121 · Outlines burnt in wood, 125 ·
    Wood silhouettes, 128

7   PHOTOGRAPHS AS TROPHIES   133
    Composition and hints, 133

8   SPECIAL TROPHIES   142
    Fish heads preserved, 142 · Fish tails preserved, 145 ·
    Head mounts, 146 · Bills or spears of big fishes, 148 ·
    Shark jaws, 153 · Letter openers from bills, 156

9   AMATEUR FISH MUSEUMS   159
    Collecting the fishes, 161 · Preserving the fishes, 165 ·
    Preserving in the field, 168 · Jars for specimen display,
    169 · Organization of fish exhibits, 170

10 FISHES IN MUSEUMS OF NATURAL HISTORY   .   .   172
    History of museum preparation, 183 · Criteria for mu-
    seum fish mounts, 185 · Museum field work, 188 · Big-
    game fishes, 198

11 REPAIRING FISH MOUNTS   200
    Fins, 200 · Head, 201 · Body, 202

12 MATERIALS AND FORMULAS   203
    Plaster of Paris, 204 · Sisal, 204 · Woven glass, 204 ·
    Conduit pipe, 204 · Plastics and resins, 205 · Formalin,
    206 · Sterine, 208 · Alum, 208 · Glycerin, 208 · Asbes-
    tos, 209 · Dextrin, 209 · Whiting, 209 · Formulas, 209

INDEX   213

HOW TO MAKE
FISH MOUNTS

1
Field Care of Fishes

Planning for an impressive trophy must start the moment the fish is landed. A few simple precautions at this stage can make all the difference between a first-class mount and a mess. None of these steps is difficult or complicated, but I have found from long experience that they will repay a little extra effort.

Color Photos and Notes

A clear photographic color transparency is an invaluable reference item in the production of any type of fish mount. A fish loses its true color immediately after death; it should be photographed while still alive or as soon as it comes out of the water. If the fish is not thoroughly exhausted and won't pose quietly, hit it smartly on the head. Often, a rap of this kind will bring out a burst of extra vivid color which the fish would not display otherwise—but be ready with your camera because this is a momentary reaction. I have found that a 35-mm. camera is best for photographic work of this type; it does not require much room in a pocket or tackle box. Take a shot of the entire fish; fill the camera finder with it. Then, as close as possible, take individual shots of the head, body, fins, and tail. Also, turn the fish on its belly and photograph its topside; then repeat for a belly shot. Take at least two different exposures of every shot to insure color perfection in the film.

3

Place the fish on the dock, bottom of the boat, or ground. Look through the finder and note that light is reflected from the surface of the fish to the camera—unless it's a very cloudy day. This reflection must be eliminated, or most of the true color will be lost. Twist and turn the camera slightly; move a foot or so in different directions. An angle to photograph the fish without reflections, or at least a minimum of reflection, can always be found. This procedure is not difficult, and with a bit of practice results should be good. If a camera is not available when the fish is caught, a later shot will of course be of some value even though the vividness of color is gone. In this case, supplement the camera work with written notes as soon as you can obtain pencil and paper.

It is possible to get by with only a field sketch and color notes if you do not have a camera. I prefer to photograph the fish and then supplement this action with copious notes on a sketch pad which contains an outline of the fish. If you know what species are to be collected, sketch a rough outline of the fishes at home, using a reference book. It will save time in the field. In recording notes an outline sketch of the fish will facilitate the recording of color without confusion. The outline need not be absolutely accurate; but the eye, lips, and all fins must be there. Jot the notes on the body of the fish sketch where the colors occur, or else put them around the drawing with a line drawn to the particular part of the fish described.

Protecting the Specimen

Protecting the specimen in the field will save much extra work later, whether the fish is intended for a skin mount or a cast. Whenever I'm collecting fish for mounting, I bring along a couple of burlap sacks. As soon as the desirable specimen is taken, the sack is soaked in water and wrapped around the fish. Two things are accomplished. First, the fish is kept cool and moist so that drying or shriveling of the skin and fins is prevented. Second, the fins are protected from damage and no scales are lost. Above all, the intended mount should not be placed on a stringer. The body of the fish will rub against the stringer, another fish, or the side of the boat; thus, irreparable damage will be done to the skin or scales. Further, the lips will tear, and repair work will be necessary when it could have been avoided. If a sack is not handy, wet grass, leaves, or weeds can

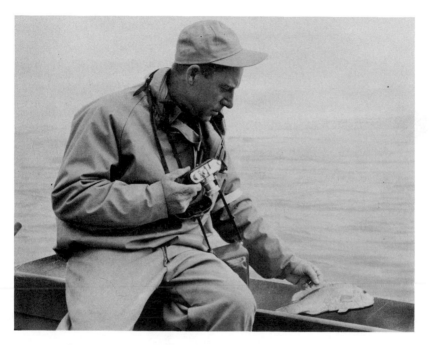

Fig. 1. Photograph the fish in color while it is still alive (a cunner). (Nova Scotia film bureau)

be used to cover the fish on all sides. A spot in the shade, protected from the sun, should be selected for temporary storage of the fish.

Even if nothing more than a silhouette trophy is desired, the fish should be protected in the same manner. A specimen which is dried by exposure to the sun or air will shrink and lose some of its natural features.

Preventing Spoilage

Obviously, the angler's first concern, after the day's fishing, should be the prevention of spoilage to his intended mount. This can be accomplished by freezing or the use of Formalin. If both these methods prove to be unsatisfactory, the angler should skin his fish in the field and salt the skin thoroughly.

Freezing. If time allows, the best method is to freeze the fish and keep it frozen until time for skinning or molding in plaster. Be sure to wrap the specimen in wet material before placing it in the freezer. The first layer should be a smooth-textured cloth, dripping with water. Any rough material will press irregularities into the fish's body which freeze that way and are difficult to remove when the fish thaws out. Do *not* bind the cloth with twine or cord because this will also mark the body. Allow the cloth to extend an inch or two beyond the tail so that the end of the tail will be protected from bending when you fold back the excess cloth. Now place the wrapped fish on a wet potato sack and fold the sack around it. This heavy, wet sack will supply additional moisture and protection for the fish when it freezes into a solid package. Again, be careful not to fold the end of the tail. Finally, wrap the whole thing in heavy wax paper which meat markets use for wrapping purposes. Bind the paper with pieces of tape, such as Scotch tape, so that the package will not unwrap.

During the procedure of wrapping the fish, its "show side" should be kept in mind because the opposite side must be down when placing the specimen in the freezer. Usually, the "down side" will flatten a bit, and this will make for difficulties in molding. Write "This side up" on the paper wrapper of the fish. Also, if possible have the fish placed on a flat surface in the freezer. All of these small details pay great dividends when it is time to mold the fish. Of course, if the fish is to be skinned, such meticulous care of the specimen is not necessary.

Arrangements for freezing specimens can usually be made with some local food store, ice cream plant, or someone who

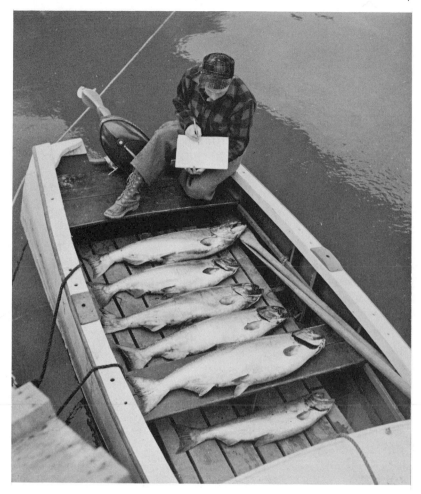

Fig. 2. Take notes on coloration and markings as soon as possible (king salmon, Alaska).

has a freezer. Surprisingly, I have always been able to do this even in tiny towns located in remote wilderness areas. If the trophy requires two or three days in transit after being frozen, or if the weather is unusually warm, it is wise to stop at an ice-cream plant or dairy where a few slabs of dry ice and a cardboard box can be purchased. One should not hesitate to do so.

Dry ice is inexpensive, and I have always found people in these plants courteous and cooperative.

During one trip from San Antonio, Texas, my wife, Bo, and I motored to Connecticut with two G.I. trunks of fish in our station wagon. My pal, Larry Sheerin, and I had flown back from a fishing trip in Mexico with snook and channel bass. Then the three of us caught largemouth bass in Texas. We froze the fish, put them in the trunks, and placed several cakes of dry ice in each trunk. At regular intervals Bo and I stopped to replenish our supply of dry ice. Our leisurely return home required several days, but we had no trouble obtaining the ice for our fish. As a matter of fact, we found it fun.

George Albrecht and I were returning from a successful trip to the Miramachi River in Canada, and with us were fine specimens of a salmon and a grilse which we intended to mount. The fish were originally frozen in the freezer of a small general store in New Brunswick. We stopped at a motel for the night and talked to the manager of the establishment concerning our fish. The manager and his wife not only accommodated our fishes in their freezer overnight but also invited us to dinner. We discovered that they were a couple of ardent fishermen. Returning from distant areas while keeping your fish frozen is a task which should not discourage any angler.

Formalin. Another method of field preservation is the use of Formalin which is a powerful chemical. It is a colorless liquid having a pungent odor with vapors that are intensely irritating to mucous membranes. Although Formalin is invaluable to scientists, both in the field and laboratory, I recommend that children do not touch it without the direct supervision of an adult. Adult anglers that can treat this chemical with respect and a bit of caution will find it advantageous for fish collection and preservation.

Before attempting this method I advise the angler to be sure to read about the use of Formalin in Chapter 12. When packing Formalin for shipment into the field, the glass jars should be well protected with excelsior, newspapers, or other material

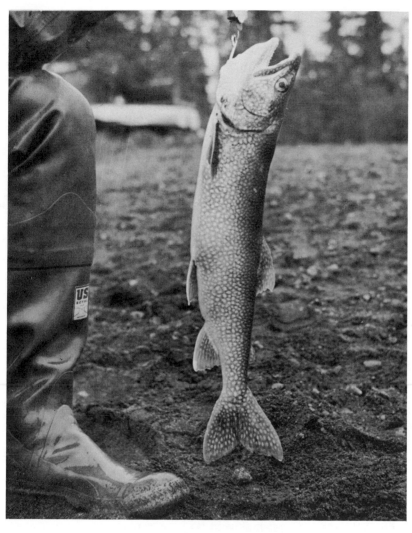

Fig. 3. In a profusely spotted fish, an enlarged black and white photo serves best as reference for the shape and size of markings (lake trout, Maine).

against breakage. I have packed Formalin for shipment to such distant places as India and Africa, and not a drop was spilled in transit although freight aboard a ship receives rough handling.

The correct solution for field preservation of fishes is nine parts water to one part Formalin. A receptacle large enough to accommodate the specimen is required. A baby's bathtub or a washtub is ideal. However, a piece of plastic cloth or any rubberized material supported on the sides with earth and stones can be formed into a suitable container. Another method is to dig a shallow rectangular pit in the ground and place the waterproof material within it; it is ready to receive the Formalin and the fish.

Before the fish is placed in the Formalin, the dorsal and anal fins should be held in lifelike positions by pins inserted at their bases. If the intended mount is to have an open mouth, it should now be pried open and a piece of wire or a twig placed in position so that the jaws will have the desired space between them. Once a fish has remained in Formalin for just a few hours, it is impossible to change the position of any part of the fish without damage. Within a day or two the fish is rigid and feels like hard rubber. Once it is preserved in position, it can be stored in Formalin in any convenient receptacle until it is time to transport it home.

A freshly caught fish should have good belly contours. If the belly is sunken, however, use a hypodermic syringe to inject full-strength (not diluted with water) Formalin into the fish's body cavity until the former roundness of the belly is recovered. If a syringe is not available, slit the abdomen along the side of the fish, opposite the show side, and fill the abdominal cavity with wet paper, cloth, moss, or any other appropriate material. The slit side of the fish should be placed down in the Formalin.

In the next day or so the specimen should be checked and two narrow strips of skin and flesh should be removed (lengthwise) from the side of the fish opposite the show side. This will facilitate penetration of the Formalin into all parts of the fish before bacterial action takes place. A big trout or bass placed in a 10 per cent solution of Formalin (nine parts water to one part

Formalin) is thoroughly preserved in a few days. However, the specimen may remain safely immersed all summer or longer.

If it is inconvenient to bring the preserved fish home in a receptacle large enough to accommodate it in Formalin, the specimen can be transported wrapped in wet cloths or wet lay-

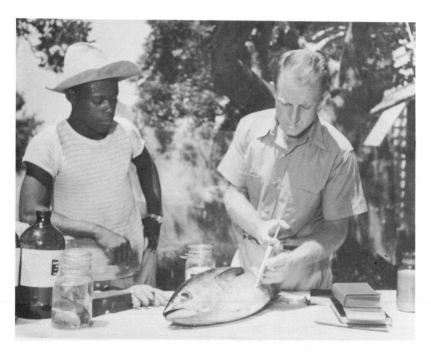

Fig. 4. If necessary, inject Formalin or water into the body cavity in order to fill it out to its full contour before molding. In warm weather, if the fish is to be left overnight, inject a 10 per cent solution of Formalin into the body cavity until the belly resumes its original shape (blackfin tuna; Walker Cay, Bahamas). (Photo by John Bennewitz)

ers of paper. Wet moss can be used also. Any wooden box will hold the fish providing a top is secured to it. A few layers of wax paper should be placed within the box so that the wood does not absorb moisture. In other words, the fish will not spoil or go soft out of the Formalin, but it is of utmost importance to keep the specimen wet so that skrinkage will not take place.

Of course, the specimen must be put back in Formalin when you get home.

When working with Formalin, water should be within easy reach in case the hands come in contact with the chemical. Reaching for a fish in Formalin—if the hands remain in the Formalin only long enough to remove the specimen—is not dangerous providing the hands are immediately washed with water. However, using rubber gloves will be safer. Formalin is extremely dangerous if splashed into the eyes accidentally. If this occurs, run fresh water into the eyes immediately. Again, do not work with Formalin if you are not familiar with it; be sure to read about Formalin in Chapter 12.

Skinning in the Field. The angler who finds it difficult to bring his trophy home in a frozen state or preserved in Formalin should skin the fish in the field before it gets soft, even if the intended mount is to be cast in plaster or in a synthetic material. In the event that a cast is desirable, the skin can be reconstructed in the home or laboratory so that a plaster mold of the fish can still be made (see Chapter 2).

For directions on field skinning read the first section on skinning in Chapter 4, then return here. But before you start the actual skinning, make a careful outline drawing of the fish on a piece of wrapping paper. Photographs or measurements of the fish, or both, will also be of assistance in reconstructing the specimen. It is easy to stray from the form of the fish in reconstruction because a fish skin will stretch or move into different positions if the original, exact contours of measurements are not employed. In order to preserve a skin in the field for future mounting, it is not necessary to clean and flesh the skin thoroughly if time is important. If there is time and it does not interfere with fishing schedules, by all means do a finished job. But the finer points of removing every bit of flesh from the skin —around the bases of the fins, tails, head bones, and cheeks— is time consuming and not necessary if the angler is rushed. This part of the job is done much better later at home and at leisure.

Salting the Skin. Thorough salting of the skin is important. Turn the skin inside out and use salt liberally around the base of the fins and tail. Rub salt well into all parts of the head, and then fill the head with another handful. Next, pile about an inch of salt over the entire fish. Turn back the sides to their original position and roll the skin into a ball, meanwhile adding still more salt. Then place another inch of salt on the bottom of a suitable container. A bait pail or a paint bucket is excellent. If a wooden box is used, place a couple of layers of wax paper around the inside. Place the rolled skin in the container and fill all the space around the fish with salt. Put the cover or lid of the container on solidly—results are best from air-tight receptacles. The box or can should not be placed in the sun or next to a heated radiator.

I have used this method on several specimens during a lengthy collecting trip in Alaska. Upon returning to the laboratory, I placed the cans containing the fish skins in the deep freeze, just as they were. Two years later I removed the specimens, and to my surprise they were excellent to work with, and the color retention of the skin amazed me. An important fish, a mahseer, was collected by me high in the mountains of Nepal— a country between Tibet and India. This salted fish skin, in an air-tight jar, traveled with me for weeks in the Himalayan Mountains and then through the heat of the Indian plains, and it arrived many months later at Yale University in excellent condition! This method should be popular with anglers because the fish skin is safe to transport and takes up little room in a car, or it can be mailed home easily without worry!

2

Plaster Molds

Once your fish has been brought away from the waterside with a minimum of damage, there are a number of different ways in which it can be transformed into a striking and decorative trophy. Perhaps the most realistic method is a cast produced from a mold of the fish's body.

Molds and Casts

A mold and a cast are not the same thing. The two are sometimes confused. A *mold* is the poured or flowed plaster which sets in a solid form around the object which is intended for reproduction. A mold may be constructed with rubber, specially mixed sands, glue, molding plaster, or other materials. In this volume we are concerned mainly with plaster molds. The *cast* is the object reproduced from the mold, a replica. In other words, a mold is the negative form from which the cast, a positive form or imitation of the original object, is reproduced.

In making fish molds use only a Grade A or No. 1 molding plaster (plaster of Paris). Stay clear of the material which is used for wall plastering. Of course, plaster should not be confused with the cement used with sand and gravel to form concrete. Molding plaster is used mostly by artists and museum workers for producing molds and casts which retain fine detail. The best grade of molding plaster, which resembles a pure white powder, is inexpensive—about $1.80 for a 100-pound bag.

Mixing the Plaster

Molding plaster must be mixed with care. Place the desired amount of water (of course the amount will vary with the size of the object to be molded) in a pan, bowl, or other receptacle. Do *not* place the plaster in the pan first. Sift the plaster into the water gradually with a scoop or trowel. Proceed to spread the plaster evenly over the entire surface of the water until the plaster no longer disappears—a light powdery layer should be obvious on the surface.

Now, roll up your sleeve and run your hand slowly through the mixture until all the plaster which remained on the surface is incorporated within. While mixing, do not work your hand in and out of the plaster, nor stir vigorously or needlessly; an excessive formation of bubbles may arise. Squeeze all lumps that may form until the entire mixture is smooth and fluid. Wipe away all bubbles which gather on the surface. The plaster is now ready for use.

Molding a Fish

Read the entire section on molding before attempting it.

A two-piece mold is usually made of any fish the size of a trout, salmon, bass, bluefish, striped bass, or perch. A one-piece mold is made when a medallion-type plaster cast is desired, when the skin is to be filled with plaster or other material, or when the fish is too large to turn over (see Chapter 10). Occasionally, an unusual job may require a mold composed of several pieces. For example, on the shores of Peru I molded a 3,300 pound-plus giant manta measuring 18½ feet from wing tip to wing tip, which required a four-piece mold. Techniques employed in the field differ slightly from those used at home or in the laboratory and will be discussed later in this section. However, let's review the basic steps first.

Remove Slime. Unless the slime is removed from the surface of the specimen, the mold will be unsatisfactory because the

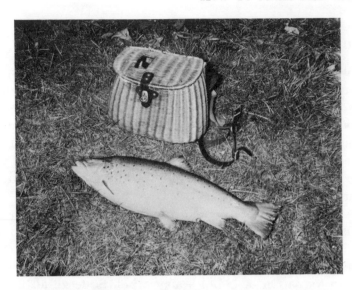

Fig. 5. Photograph your fish and take color notes before molding. This is a 12-pound brown trout taken in Connecticut.

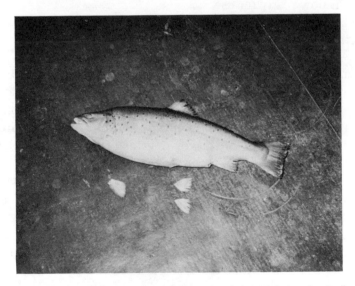

Fig. 6. The pectoral and ventral fins are cut off from the body.

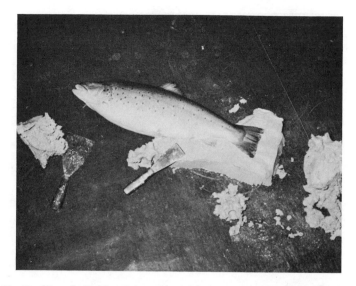

Fig. 7. Build a shelf of soil, sand, or asbestos around the fish to the mid-line of its body.

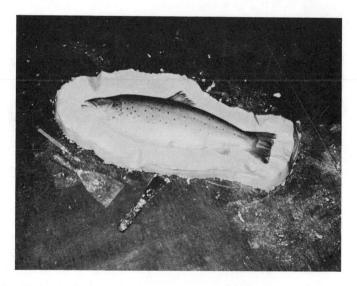

Fig. 8. Cut two V-shaped keys or recesses along each side of the shelf. This can be done now or the keys can be cut into the plaster of the first half of the mold.

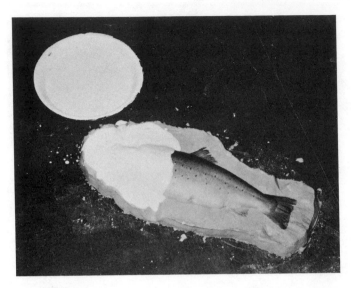

Fig. 9.   Flow the plaster over the fish.   Start at the head or tail end.

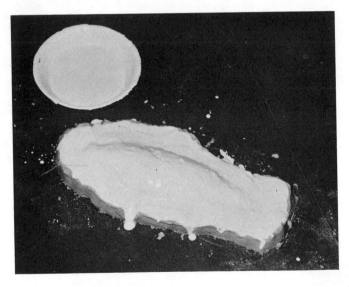

Fig. 10.   Continue until the entire fish and the shelf are covered.

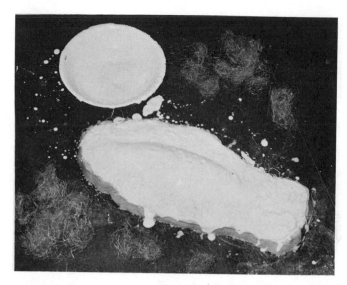

Fig. 11. Molds of large fish should be reinforced with sisal. Cover the shelf first.

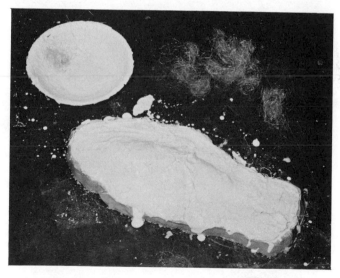

Fig. 12. Continue over the body of the fish.

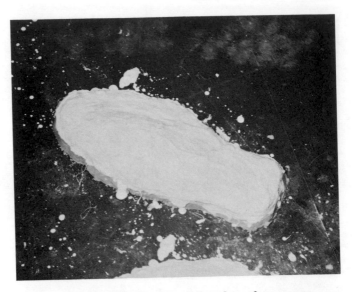

Fig. 13. Add plaster along the edges if necessary.

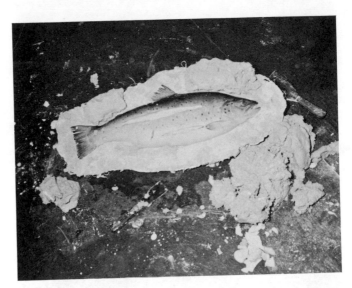

Fig. 14. When the mold has set, turn it over and remove the material
(asbestos, sand, or soil) from it.

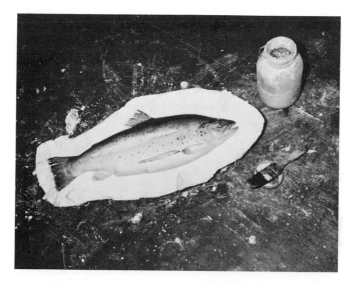

Fig. 15. Clean the shelf of the mold and apply the sterine separator.

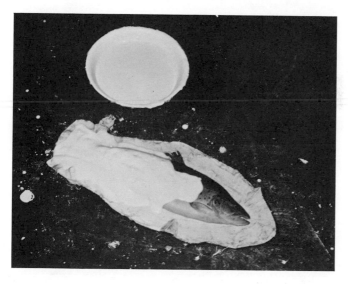

Fig. 16. Proceed with the plaster the same way on this side.

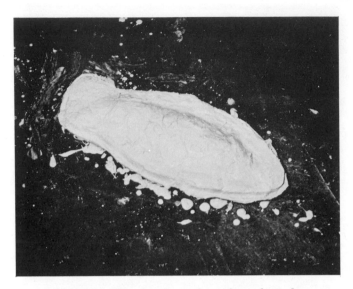

Fig. 17. Also reinforce this side with sisal.

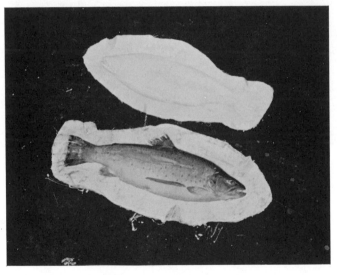

Fig. 18. When the plaster has set, insert a chisel between the halves and
pry the mold apart.

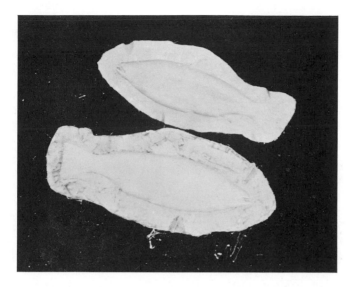

Fig. 19. Place these halves together and set aside to dry.

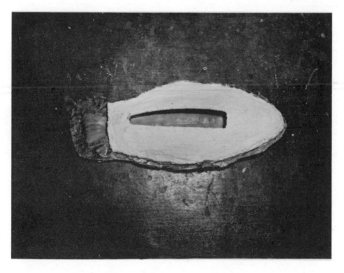

Fig. 20. The mold ready for casting. Before cutting the rear side of the
mold, as shown here, see Figs. 39 to 44.

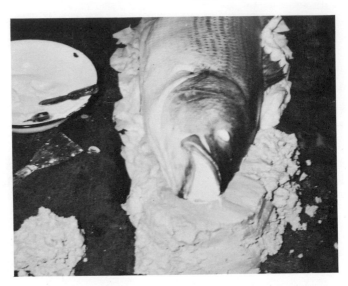

Fig. 21. To make a separate mold of the open mouth, simply push a heavy mixture of plaster into it before making a mold of the body. Allow the plaster to set. Apply sterine separator over the mold of the mouth before placing plaster on the body.

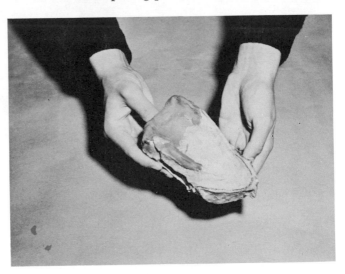

Fig. 22. The mold of the mouth. If the back end of the mold has holes or outstanding irregularities, correct them with modeling clay, as shown above.

plaster will not set solidly next to the skin and definition will be poor. This is not very important when the mold is intended for use as a form for mounting the skin, but it is extremely important when the mold will be cast. First, go over the entire fish with a brush and water. This will remove all excessive dirt and slime. Then pour about half a pint of vinegar into a quart of water and go over the whole fish. Rinse the fish well with clean water. Next, mix a handful of alum in a quart of water and again go over the fish. Pour the remaining alum water over the fish and let it remain on the specimen while preparing the next step. The alum has astringent qualities; that is, it tends to contract or bind organic tissues and helps to alleviate the problem of slime and the oozing of fluids in the skin. Another, easier method is to wipe the fish dry with a cloth and then simply spray or brush a thin coat of lacquer over the specimen. Nearly all hardware stores carry small cans of lacquer which spray by simply pressing a release button. Lacquer dries almost instantly and covers any slime on the fish. It is best to apply the lacquer to the show side when the fish is all set and positioned in plaster.

Show Side and Fins. Choose the side which will be shown in the mount (called the show side) and lay the fish down on the other side. Clip the pectoral and ventral fins close to their bases and set them aside in a glass of water so that they do not dry out. A mold of these fins will be made later. Arrange the other fins in position. This is accomplished by inserting pins or pointed wire through the forepart of the fin and anchoring well into the body. Do not stretch the fins but position them so that they look natural.

Belly Contour. Next, check the belly or abdominal contour. If it is sunken it should be filled either by an injection of water with a hypodermic syringe or by cutting a slit (opposite show side) and filling the abdominal cavity with pieces of cloth, newspaper, moss, or any other suitable material.

Shelf Around Fish. Now place the fish on a table or the ground with its show side up and build a shelf of soil, sand, or asbestos—depending on where the work is taking place—completely around it to the mid-line (Fig. 7). On a fish the size of a 15-inch bass or trout, the shelf should extend out 3 or 4 inches. Cut two V-shaped keys or recesses (Fig. 8) along each side of this shelf. Keys will facilitate easier adjoinment of the halves later. If the lacquer system is used for the slime problem, now is the time to use it. Before the plaster is mixed, the lacquer will be ready to receive the plaster.

Mold of Open Mouth. With smaller fishes the mold of the mouth can be included with the first half of the mold by simply pushing plaster into the mouth. In this case use care when removing the original fish from the mold so that the plaster, which forms the mold of the mouth, is not broken off. If it does break off, however, it can be glued back before casting the fish. After the cast is produced, the plaster in the mouth is dug out with appropriate small tools.

With a large fish, however, such as a 50-pound striped bass, it is better to make a separate mold of the mouth. Before applying plaster to the show side of the fish, push a heavy mixture of plaster well into the mouth. Allow it to set and apply sterine separator. After the mold of the whole fish has been completed, the mold of the mouth can then be separated from it.

Applying Plaster. If the plaster is mixed in a large pan, use a smaller bowl to scoop up the plaster and convey it to the specimen. Flow the plaster over the fish evenly (Fig. 9). I prefer to apply the plaster by hand. Start at either the head or tail end and continue along. Do not skip from one part of the fish to the other. Be sure the plaster flows to the edges of the shelf so that no air pockets are formed. The entire fish should be covered quickly with a thin coat, often called the "splash coat." Then, the entire shelf should be covered also. Start immediately again on one end and flow the remainder of the plaster over the entire fish. Enough plaster should be mixed in the first batch to cover the fish and the shelf to about a depth of ¾ inch. Do not disturb the mold until it sets, usually about an hour. Notice that the mold heats perceptibly before setting. This warmth can be felt by placing the hand on the mold. Never disturb the mold before this action takes place; wait until the warmth is gone.

Now turn the fish and mold over to the other side. Remove the asbestos or sand (Fig. 16) and clean the hardened plaster, which now forms a plaster shelf around the specimen. Wipe the exposed side of the fish and give it a coat of lacquer (if using this method). Apply a separator to the shelf to prevent the flowing plaster from adhering to the set plaster. The separator may be Vaseline or sterine applied with a brush. Mix another batch of plaster and repeat the process on this side of the fish.

Warning! Plaster sets fairly fast. Do not diddle along while working. Clean the plaster mixing receptacles as soon as possible. First remove as much plaster as you can with your hand; then use a scrub brush and water to remove the thin layer remaining—but quickly!

Molding the Fins. While the mold is setting the pectoral fin and the two ventral fins, which were cut off earlier, can be attended to. Simply place them on a piece of glass, table top, or other smooth surface which has been greased with Vaseline or sterine separator. Flow the plaster over the fins. The three fins can be incorporated in one mold, but I prefer to mold each separately (Fig. 23). When the plaster has set, turn the molds over and cut two or three keys into the plaster of each mold (Fig. 26). Apply the separator and flow the plaster over the half molds thus making them each two piece. When the plaster has set, insert a chisel between the halves and tap gently with a hammer; the halves will separate. Remove the fins and set aside the molds to dry.

Separating Mold Halves. Now return to the fish mold, and check that it has set. Separate the halves by inserting a chisel here and there between the two parts. The halves should come apart easily unless an excessive amount of plaster was allowed to flow down over the first half of the mold during the plastering of the second part. If this is the case, the edges have to be

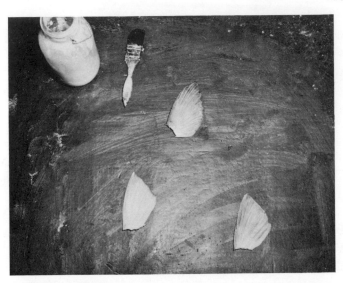

Fig. 23. The pectoral and ventral fins of a striped bass ready for molding. Brush sterine over the table top first so that the plaster will not adhere to it.

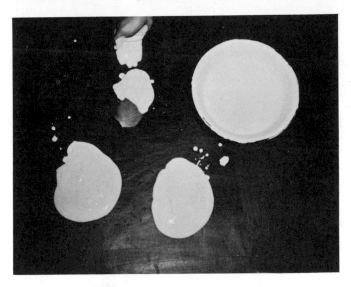

Fig. 24. Cover each fin with plaster.

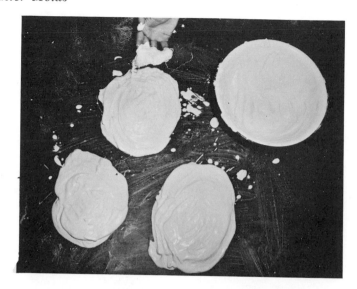

Fig. 25. Molds of large fins should be reinforced with sisal.

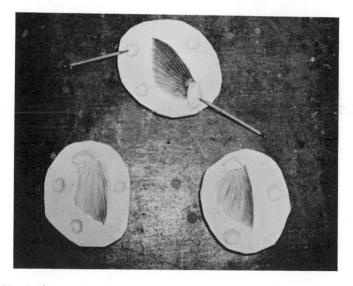

Fig. 26. Left pencil points to a conelike key which has been gouged out of the plaster. The right pencil points to the gouged out area at the base of the fin; it will provide for an extension of the fin when it is cast. Do not remove the fins. Brush sterine over the mold and then apply plaster.

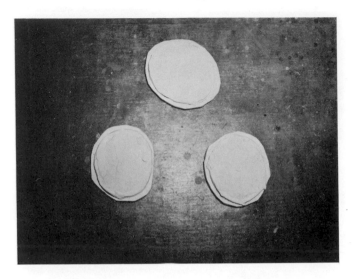

Fig. 27. A two-piece mold is made.

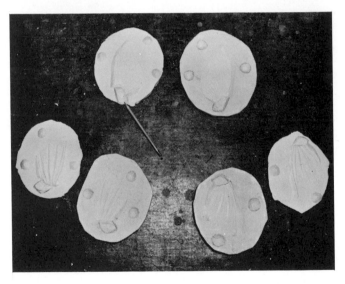

Fig. 28. The mold halves are separated and fins removed. Pencil
points to the protruding area at the fin base which has to be cut away
level with the shelf of the mold.

scraped until the line of demarcation can be seen clearly between the halves. Insert the chisel again and the mold halves will part cleanly.

Remove the fish without damaging the mold detail. I usually start by carefully inserting a fingernail under a corner of the tail fin and then gradually pull the fish's body up and toward the head. Clear away any bits of plaster on and around the shelves of the mold that might prevent the halves from coming together snugly. Place the halves together and set the mold aside until dried and ready for casting. As a protection, I always tie wire around each end of the mold so that nosey people will not open it and run their fingernails over the inside. A mold set over a furnace will dry quickly. During summer when furnaces are shut off, the mold should be placed outdoors or in a room with open windows. The fish cannot be cast unless the mold has lost most of its moisture. A fish mold 2 or 3 feet long should be dry enough within two or three days if placed over a furnace or in a heated room.

Molding in the Field

Molding techniques in the field and at home or in the laboratory are basically the same, but through years of trial and error I have found modifications in the process which are advantageous in each situation. The best possible results in the eventual cast are obtained from a mold which is completed as soon as possible after the fish is caught, and that means the same day or the next morning. This method is a must for scientific museum workers, and more information on it is found in Chapter 10. However, an angler who is vacationing and lives in a tent, cabin, or cottage, not too far from shore, may try a hand at field molding during the lull of the fishing day.

Select a spot in the shade, if possible, for the temporary laboratory. Fresh water is necessary. If a faucet is not handy, fill a barrel or some 5-gallon tins with water from a distant water tap or from the lake and transport the water to the spot where the work is to take place.

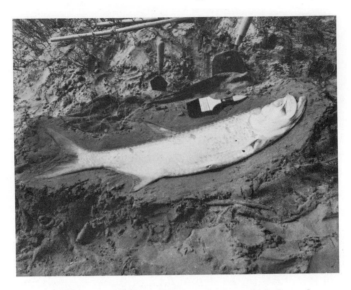

Fig. 29. A tarpon in the Florida Keys is being molded. A base or shelf of sand is built up around the fish to the mid-line of the body. The exposed side of the tarpon is the "show side."

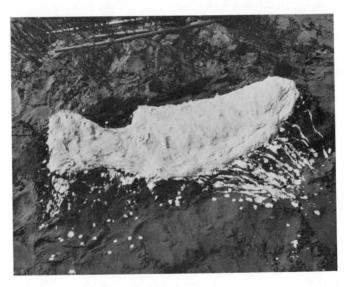

Fig. 30. A layer of plaster and then sisal and plaster are applied as in Figs. 9 to 13.

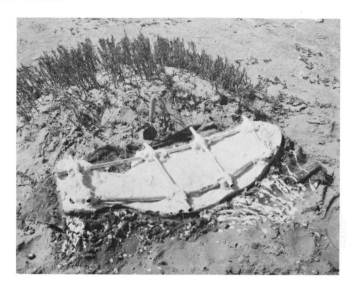

Fig. 31. The mold is reinforced with thin wall conduit or other pipe.

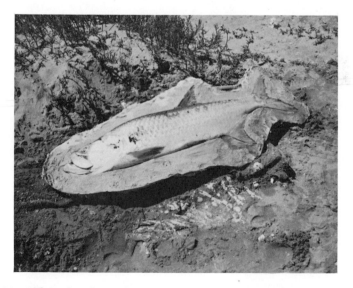

Fig. 32. When the plaster has set, the mold is turned over (with the fish in it); and the second half of the mold is made in the same manner as the first.

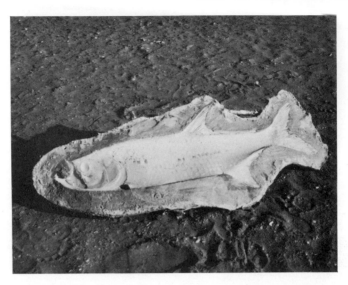

Fig. 33. A close-up of the show side of the mold.

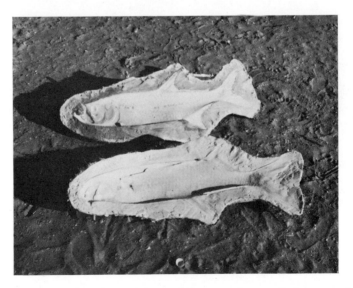

Fig. 34. Clean the edges of the molds; wire the two halves together so
that the insides won't get damaged.

Find some soil fairly free from rocks and debris for the shelf around the fish. Add enough water to the soil so that it will remain where placed (Fig. 29). A seashore beach is an excellent spot for this type of work. Plenty of salt water is at hand to mix with the sand, and the plaster bowls can be cleaned easily directly in the surf. Remember, though that, fresh water is still necessary for mixing the plaster.

The advantage of working out of doors is that the plaster bowls can be cleaned without fuss, and any excess plaster can be dumped on a pile. And of course there is no worry of decorating the floor, walls, or furniture with plaster! The actual molding of the fish is followed in the same manner as described in the forepart of this section.

If the mold is to be transported some distance, it is advisable to add sisal for strength. Dip a handful of this fiber in plaster and place it over the first coat of plaster until the entire fish and shelf are covered. An added precaution is the placement of pipe along the sides and across the mold (Fig. 31). For further details read Chapter 10.

Molding at Home

Although more care has to be exercised while working with plaster at home or in the laboratory, there are many advantages of convenience which cannot be had in the field. Fresh water is at hand, the sun cannot dry out the specimen, and wind is not present to blow sand over it.

A frozen specimen must first be thawed out. If the fins are dry, do not attempt to place them in position until they have been soaked in water. Wrap wet cloths or wet paper towels around the fins and the tail, or place the entire fish in water. When the fins are soft, prepare the fish as previously described.

If you have been able to bring home only the skin, proceed as follows to build the body out to its former contours for molding. Fill the head and skin with ground gray asbestos which has been mixed with water to a putty-like consistency. Sew the skin together partially; then add or remove asbestos. Finish sewing the skin, turn the fish over carefully, and proceed to model the fish to its original proportions. Use the outline tracing and photos of the fresh fish.

Either of two methods can be used to mold a fish indoors— choice is a matter of personal preference. One way is to build a temporary, shallow, rectangular box, about the height of a mold. Grease the inside of the box or line it with wax paper so that the set plaster will not adhere to the wood. Pour the plaster into the receptacle until it reaches half way up the sides of the box. Place the fish on the plaster carefully. Press the specimen here and there into the plaster until the plaster is forced to the mid-line of the fish's back and the mid-line of the belly. Be careful not to allow plaster to flow over the face-up side of the fins and tail; if it does, the plaster can be scraped away when it starts to set. As the plaster begins to harden, cut some round conelike keys along the sides or the shelf of the mold. After the plaster has set, apply the separator and pour the other side. Pour the plaster slowly, starting at one end, and be careful not to lock in air pockets with plaster.

The other way of molding indoors is to construct a shelf around the fish the same way as when working in the field. Instead of sand or soil, however, use asbestos—a clean, pleasant material which can be worked many times over and over again. I use ground gray asbestos which is inexpensive. A 50-pound bag will be sufficient for any trout, bass, or bluefish. Mix the asbestos with water until it reaches a smooth consistency and can be troweled. Do not mix too much water with the asbestos or it will not stay put. Place the asbestos in a bowl, and add water to it gradually while mixing it by hand. With a little prac- tice the asbestos can be shaped perfectly around the fish (Fig. 7). When finished with the job, dump the wet asbestos in a 5- gallon pail which has a cover. If the asbestos has dried after being stored away for a few months, simply add water, let it soak a while, and then work the asbestos with both hands until it becomes soft.

With a bit of care plaster can be used at home in the basement or workroom without making a mess. A piece of glass on the table top can facilitate neat work. Rub some grease over the glass so that plaster can be scraped up easily. Layers of newspapers can be used or a table top can be greased. Have a waste bucket handy to accommodate whatever plaster is left over in the mixing bowl. If the plaster receptacles are to be cleaned in the sink, be sure to remove as much plaster as possible first. Then, run some water into the bowl and work the sides well with a scrub brush or some rough material such as excelsior or steel wool. During this process be sure the tap water is going, otherwise the plaster sediment may accumulate in the sink trap and stop up the drain system. I have been cleaning plaster bowls in sinks for many years and have yet to experience any trouble with the drainage of the sinks. However, if in doubt, or if mother or the good wife frowns on this procedure, the plaster bowl can be cleaned in a tub of water. And later, after pouring off the water, the remaining plaster in the bottom of the tub, which will not harden, may be disposed of outdoors in the trash can.

3
Casts

The cast or mount is reproduced from the plaster mold. Fishes can be cast satisfactorily in four mediums: plaster of Paris, wax, casting compound, and synthetic or plastic materials. I do not advise the use of latex or other rubber-like substances for mounts or casts that are to be permanent. Within a few years the rubber hardens and cracks, and the paint begins to peel from it.

PREPARING THE MOLD FOR CASTING

If one side of the mold was cracked during transit or otherwise damaged so that it is no longer one rigid piece, repair it in this manner. Place the two halves together with the damaged side facing up. Check to see that the halves fit together snugly. Sponge water onto the area about the crack or cracks. This is necessary—otherwise the dry mold will suck out moisture from the new plaster applied and results will be unsatisfactory. Mix a pan of plaster and dip pieces of tow, sisal fiber, or excelsior in it. Apply these "hunks" of plaster-fiber liberally over the cracked or broken surface. Do not disturb the mold until the plaster used in repair is completely set. Of course, a one-piece mold can be repaired by using the same techniques.

Usually, a one-piece mold is used for casting fishes in plaster. Wax casts can be reproduced from a one- or two-piece mold,

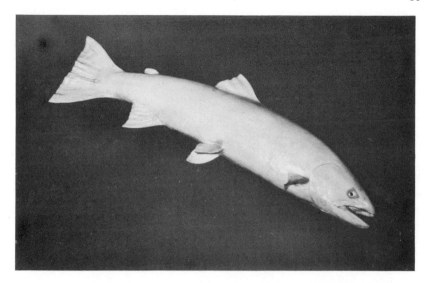

Fig. 35. Cast of a steelhead ready for painting.

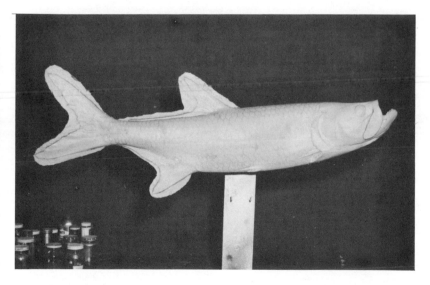

Fig. 36. Cast of a tarpon. The next step is to saw off areas around fins.

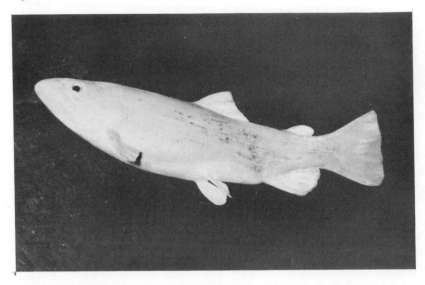

Fig. 37. Cast of a brown trout ready for painting.

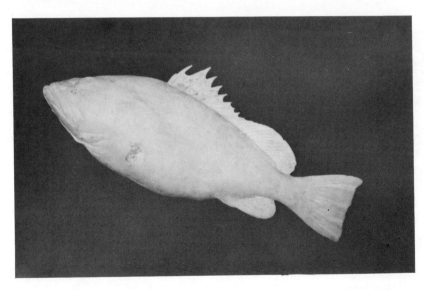

Fig. 38. Cast of a Nassau grouper. The next step is to drill out holes to accommodate fins.

depending on where and how the mounts are to be displayed. Casts in compound or in plastics require a two-piece mold to reproduce a whole fish.

All molds require attention and preparation, however, before the casting medium can be applied. The mold should be thoroughly dry. If sand or asbestos has been used for the shelf in producing the mold, all bits of loose material should be swept out of the hollow impression by gently using a 2-inch paint brush. The shelves of the mold can be swept with a scrubbing brush.

Show Side of Mold

The show side of the mold is that half which will reproduce the show side of the fish. If the mold is intended for reproducing a mount in plastic or casting compound, give it a preliminary thin coat of shellac. This preliminary coat will make it easier to detect small holes or pockets caused by air bubbles, foreign material, or damage. Fill these defects with modeling clay or small pieces of wax. If necessary, model the repaired surface with an appropriate tool. Sometimes the detail of the lips or parts of the head in the mold may be broken off when removing the original fish from the mold. Now is the time to model in any detail that might have been snapped off.

Now, apply another coat of shellac, thinned 50–50 with alcohol, to the mold. When this has dried, apply yet another coat. Several brushings of shellac will be required until the mold begins to acquire a gloss. The next step is to apply the separator —formula No. 6 (see Chapter 12). The mold is now ready for casting.

Rear Half of Mold

In a two-piece mold the rear half reproduces the back portion of the fish, the side that goes against the wall. With a soft pencil or crayon, outline the areas of the mold that are to be sawed off or chipped away (Fig. 39). In the illustration the line

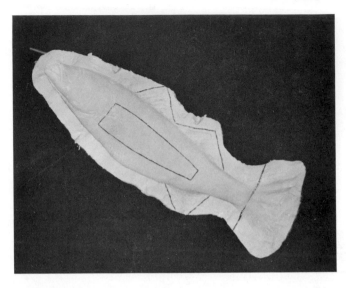

Fig. 39. Outline the areas of the mold which are to be sawed off or chipped away.

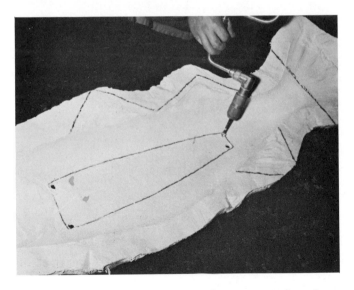

Fig. 40. Drill holes in the four corners with a countersink tool to accommodate the saw.

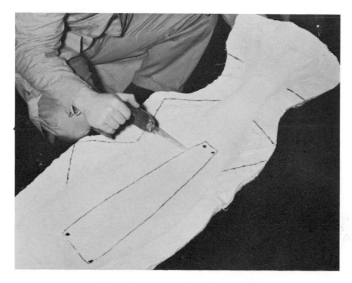

Fig. 41. Use a key-hole saw.

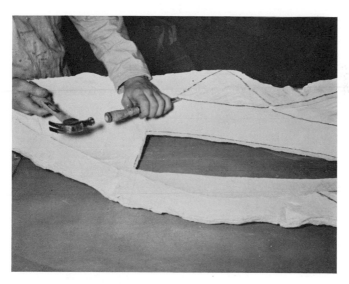

Fig. 42. Chip away the fin areas to a depth of about ½ inch.

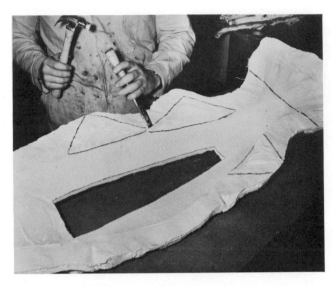

Fig. 43. Chip away around the dorsal and anal fins—about an inch beyond the edge of the impression of the fin.

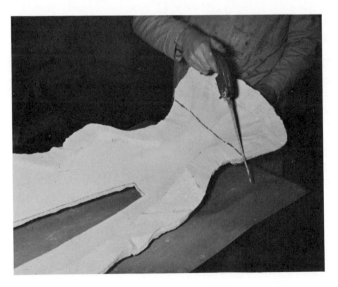

Fig. 44. Saw off the tail.

just before the tail indicates where the mold is sawed off complete. The oblong-shaped outline is a guide to the area to be
sawed from this side of the mold. Use a key-hole saw. Drill
holes in the four corners with a countersink tool to accommodate the saw (Fig. 40).

The lines around the dorsal and anal fins—about an inch
beyond the edge of the impression of the fin—indicates the areas
that are chipped away to a depth of about ½ inch. The reason
for removing these areas is to accommodate the cast fins which
have to be thicker than the originals. There must be room for
them when the mold halves are placed together; otherwise, the
halves of the mold will not come together snugly. The entire
process is demonstrated in Figs. 39 to 44.

Shellac the mold and apply separator in the same way as for
the show side. Further treatment of the molds for the individual
methods is included in the following sections.

CASTS IN PLASTER

The easiest, quickest, and least expensive method of producing a cast is to do it in plaster (molding plaster No. 1). Only a
one-side mold is necessary, and no preliminary coat of shellac is needed. The cast can be made into a medallion type,
which includes a plaque cast as one piece with the fish; or the
plaque can be eliminated. Let us consider the medallion type
first. Place the mold in a pan of water (if the mold is too large,
run water over it) until it is thoroughly wet. This requires only
a few minutes. (A saturated mold will not draw moisture from
the fresh plaster of the cast, and saturation helps in eliminating
bubble holes in the cast.) Remove the mold from the water
when air bubbles are no longer released from the plaster. Get
rid of any drops of water in the mold with a paper towel or a
cloth. Apply the sterine separator to the entire mold, including
the shelf. Rub your fingers gently over the mold as a check
to smooth out any sterine that might have been applied to
excess.

Flow the plaster into the hollow of the mold, starting at one end. Let the hollow fill first; then allow the plaster to run onto the shelf of the mold. Now wait until the plaster starts setting a bit and reaches a heavy whipped-cream-like consistency. Trowel enough plaster over all until a thickness of about ¾ inch is evident on the shelf of the mold. In other words, the plaque will be constructed of plaster ¾ inch thick. If the fish is more than 14 to 16 inches in length, the plaque can be reinforced with tow or sisal dipped in plaster. Insert two pieces of looped

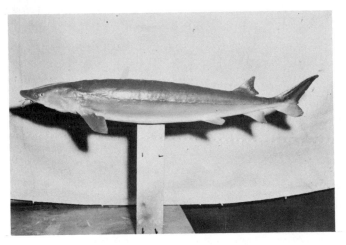

Fig. 45. Sturgeon cast in plaster.

wire into the back of the cast while the plaster is still soft. Turn the ends so that the wire will not pull out. These loops will serve as eye-hooks to hold a wire for hanging purposes. Another method is to insert a looped wire into the center of the top edge of the plaque.

Run a trowel or a knife along the edge of the cast before the plaster is set. It is easier to obtain a clean, smooth edge in this manner rather than by hacking away at the hard cast when it is removed from the mold.

A mold that is to be used for a plaster cast should be made thin and without sisal or tow reinforcements so that it can be chipped away easily from the cast. A small ¼-inch chisel and a light hammer should be used. The addition of color, such as bluing, to the water when mixing plaster for either the mold or the cast will be a help in differentiating one from the other during the chipping process. Damage to the cast, by the chisel biting in too deeply, will be lessened because it will be clearly seen where the mold stops and the cast begins.

The pectoral and ventral fins can be reproduced separately in plaster, but I do not advise it; plaster fins, extending outward from the body, are too fragile. It is preferable to replace these

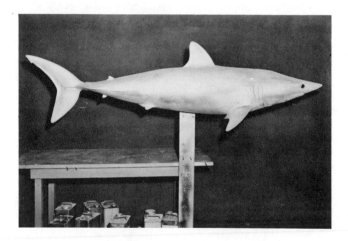

Fig. 46. Mako shark cast in plaster.

fins with artificial ones carved (a small electrical grinding tool is best) from sheet Celluloid or other plastic-like material. For this method, cut the original fins from the body before molding; then trace their outline onto the Celluloid with a sharp tool and cut them out. A simpler method is to fold the fins against the body, therefore including them in the mold. In other words, the pectoral and ventral fins can be reproduced in plaster just as they appeared folded against the body.

If the cast is to appear as a whole fish, without a back or plaque, avoid flowing the plaster onto the shelf of the mold except in the areas containing the impressions of the tail and fins. When the plaster starts to thicken, trowel more of it over the cast—about ¾ inch over the body and about ½ inch over the tail and dorsal and anal fins. Insert wires into the back of the fish as described previously. Or the cast can be placed directly against the wall (no space between wall and fish) by eliminating the wires. Instead, carve out a hole in the back of the cast and insert a piece of metal or wire across the top end of the hole while the plaster is still soft. With this method the fish plaque can be placed on a nail or hook snug against the wall.

When the cast has been separated from the mold, carve out the eye area to the proper depth to receive the glass eye with room to spare. Brush shellac into the hollow. When the shellac dries run some hot wax into the hole and then insert the glass eye. Smooth the wax around the eye with a tool. An easy way of applying the wax is to heat any small metal tool and touch it to a piece of beeswax held directly over the eye impression. Let the wax drop into it.

Now check over the cast and fill in any defects with plaster or wax; if plaster is used first, wet the area to be repaired. Scrape away any irregularities in the plaque. Chisel or cut away any bits of plaster that may be attached to the fish. The lips, jaws, and gill cover may require deeper lines; cut them in with a knife or other pointed instrument.

If the fish has been cast without the plaque, bevel the edges of the body and fins from their outer edge inward toward the back of the fish. In this way the fish will appear to be fully cast when hung upon the wall.

Cover the entire cast with shellac thinned 50–50 with commercial alcohol and apply several coats until the cast begins to hint of gloss. Paint the fish (see Chapter 5).

CASTS IN WAX

The wax cast is another method of casting fish which may be accomplished at home easily and at minimum expense. In certain instances casting in wax is superior to any other means of constructing models of fishes. It is the simplest and fastest method of obtaining many reproductions out of the same mold. For example, in museum display groups a school of fishes, which usually travel with their age-mates of the same size, can all be produced from the same mold. It is a simple matter to warm the individual casts in hot water so that their bodies can be turned here and there to make them look slightly different one from another. Wax fish can be cast in a half mold, which is usually sufficient when constructing a school of fishes where only one side will be seen, or the whole fish can be cast using a two-piece mold. A wax cast is not fragile, nor is it a messy job if done properly.

Wax Casts—Half Mold

Let us assume first that only the show side of the fish will be cast. Immerse the mold in hot water. If the mold is too large for a tub or the sink, pour hot water over it. The mold should be soaked at least until all the air bubbles are released from it. In other words, the mold has absorbed all the water it can.

A separating medium is required between the plaster mold and the wax cast—as it is necessary in all casting processes. However, a different, simple separator is used. Before applying wax to the mold, soap it well with a thin solution of green surgical soap or shaving soap; or the usual soap powder or soap flakes used in the kitchen may be brushed dry onto the wet mold until a heavy lather forms. Remove the lather with a brush. Run the brush in the mold and wipe it on a cloth or towel after every few strokes. Sweep the brush over the mold until a slight polished effect is obtained. A thin film of soap will be left on the surface of the mold which will facilitate the separation of the wax cast from the plaster mold. If the wax is too hot when applied to the mold, however, difficulty will be experienced in separating the two. I have found that oil, Vaseline, lard, etc., are not satisfactory separators.

A fish reproduced in wax can be made as durable as plaster if it is handled with care. But any wax used in an unadulterated form in casting is unsatisfactory because either it is too brittle or the melting point is low. It is difficult to work a cast which is brittle; and it would prove embarrassing if, on a hot summer's day, when you were proudly displaying a wax-cast trophy to a friend, the fish's jaws began to droop and its tail began to sag. Therefore, a small portion of another type of wax such as carnauba is added to inexpensive paraffin wax. The carnauba wax brings the composition to a higher melting point.

Other qualities desirable in a wax casting compound are toughness, bending without breaking, and no warping or crack-

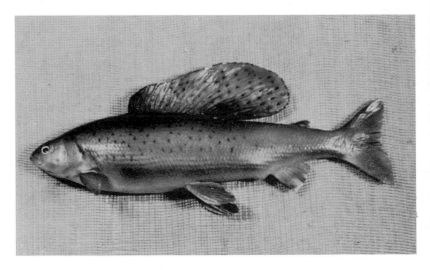

Fig. 47. Grayling cast in wax.

ing. Common rosin, which is the resin of a pine tree and often called colophony, added to the wax in a correct amount does the job. It also causes the composition to harden more slowly and thus prevents cracking to a great extent. For the correct preparation of this casting wax, see section on formulas (Chapter 12).

Anyone interested in using wax as a casting medium may come across many different formulas. The individual formulas may be composed of different types of wax—all of which have about the same melting point. The addition of several kinds of wax only complicates the matter and means nothing. Many workers with wax add substances such as whiting, talc, and plaster of Paris to the wax. Why? I don't know. These substances only act as fillers and accomplish nothing except to change the color of the composition. Also, when a filler such as whiting is added in excessive quantity, the resulting composition becomes brittle and may even crumble. Stay with the simple formula found in Chapter 12. Fillers are justified when certain effects such as metal, stone, and wood are desired. The angler

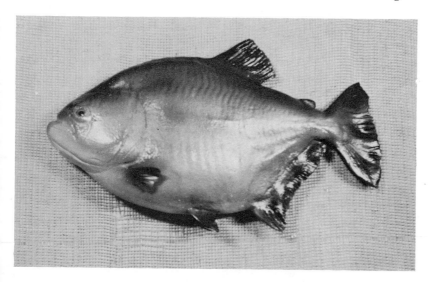

Fig. 48. Piranha cast in wax.

may find it interesting to experiment by adding powdered glass, marble meal, or metallic powders such as copper, silver, or gold.

Two methods can be used in applying the wax composition to the mold—brushing or pouring. If the mold is fairly small and has been heated in hot water, pouring wax into the mold will be satisfactory. Brushing the wax into the mold, however, has many advantages. The mold does not have to be lifted and tilted back and forth in an attempt to place the wax in the same thickness over the entire mold. There is less chance of border lines forming as the wax cools during the process of tilting the mold. It is more economical because there is no loss of wax over the sides, and the cast is of uniform thickness throughout.

As soon as the mold is taken out of the hot water, apply the soap quickly so that the mold remains warm during the application of wax. No drops of water should be in the mold; dab them out with a piece of cotton. Now pour or brush in the hot wax. If pouring, tilt the mold from side to side so that the wax will reach all parts and crevices. Pour the excess wax back into the pot. Repeat the process immediately, and repeat again until the cast has attained a thickness of about ⅛ to ¼ inch. Before removing the cast from the mold, it should be reinforced with two or three layers of gauze which have first been dipped in the pot of wax. (Include the tail and fins in the reinforcement process unless the wax fins will be replaced with fins constructed out of Celluloid or other plastic material.) Brush more wax onto the gauze until it is well impregnated with wax. Be sure the wax is hot enough to penetrate the gauze completely so that it will stick to the surface beneath the gauze; otherwise, the gauze will act as a separating medium between the two layers of wax.

Absorbent cotton can be used instead of the gauze. First, spread a thin layer of cotton over the entire cast including fins and tail, and then brush the wax over the cotton. If the cast needs to be strengthened even more, this can be accomplished by applying plaster of Paris. Dip gauze, tow, strips of loose burlap, or other fibrous material into the plaster and apply it to the cast.

If brushing wax into the mold (the better method) instead of pouring, use a small varnish brush. Of course, bring the pot of wax to the mold so that the brush can be dipped quickly from the pot to the mold. Reinforce the brushed cast the same way as the poured cast.

As a base for inserting screw eyes or hooks for hanging purposes, place a piece of wood in back of the cast and anchor it with cotton dipped in hot wax. A couple of nails tapped into the sides of the wood so that their heads protrude about an inch will provide good spots to attach the cotton. The cotton can be placed in position dry, and then the wax can be applied with a brush. If the mold is intended to be immersed in hot water to facilitate the removal of the wax cast, the wood should be waterproofed with hot wax before securing it in the cast.

When brushing the wax into the mold, extend the wax over the edge of the hollow impression of the mold and beyond the edges of the fins and tail for about ½ inch. This will facilitate removal of the cast from the mold by supplying an area to pry under without damage to the cast. Sometimes, especially if there are undercuts in the plaster mold, the cast will not separate easily. In this case, the mold can be warmed just enough to bend the wax slightly, here and there, so that it can be removed from the mold without damage. Then, the fish should be pressed back into shape before the wax cools completely.

Upon the removal of the cast or positive form from the mold, tiny defects in the surface, usually caused by gas bubbles, may be apparent. The defects and any other blemishes can be corrected by filling in these areas with a pastelike mixture which is made in the following manner. Pour a small amount of the wax composition into a glass jar with a screw-type top. Add a few drops of turpentine to the melted wax. This will bring down the melting point of the wax and make it pliable after setting. Place the top on the jar. Shake it well until the wax and the turpentine are mixed. Before using this paste, place the jar in warm water to soften the contents. Use a sculptor's wooden tool, or any other similar device, to apply and model the paste onto the cast. Eventually, the turpentine dries or evaporates; and the repaired area becomes as hard as the rest of the cast. The repaired areas should have a day or two to dry and harden. Before painting the cast, apply a thin coat of shellac over the entire fish.

It is not necessary to use the wax composition for repairing if a job must be done in a hurry. Regular putty can be substituted, although the repair job will not be as good. The putty can be colored to match the rest of the cast—if that is desired— by adding pigment (oil color) just as it comes out of the tube. If this makes the putty too sticky, add some whiting or dry plaster of Paris.

If the fish is to be painted with oil or lacquer colors, a thin coat of shellac (thinned 50–50 with alcohol) should be applied first. Otherwise, the surface of the cast may soften because of contact of the oil, turpentine, or lacquer medium with the wax of the cast. The best substance to use for shellacking is the clear yellow liquid that rises to the surface of a jar of white shellac on standing. This light yellow liquid should be diluted with three parts alcohol before using.

Wax Casts—Full Mold

If the whole fish is to be cast (rather than one side), a two-piece mold is used. Cut an oblong section out of the back side of the mold and saw off the tail section as described in Chapter 3. Proceed to brush in the wax and reinforcements as described previously. Remove the casts from both sides of the mold. With tools such as knives, mounted razor blades, scalpels, or wood-carver chisels, trim the edges of the casts which overlapped the edges of the molds. Trim the halves so that they fit together perfectly. One method of cementing two pieces of a wax cast together is to heat a knife blade over a flame and then draw it between the two pieces. The wax on both edges will melt, and as the wax cools the edges will bind. The two pieces must be pressed together firmly while the knife is being drawn between them. Also, they should be held together long enough after that to allow the wax to cool and thus set. Another way is to trim the edges of the halves, place them together, and then apply a hot tool in a few spots inside so that the two pieces are held in place. Then clinch the halves together permanently by applying cotton dipped in hot wax to the seam. Gauze dipped in hot wax can be used also. Brush more wax over the seam area if necessary. If the fish cast is to be screwed to a plaque, place a piece of wood in the cast and secure it with cotton and hot wax.

A wax cast of a fish can be bent into a different position by simply placing it in a pan of warm water. Do not rush the job because the cast cracks easily if it has not warmed enough. If a fin or tail is to be curved, it is not necessary to immerse the entire cast.

Fins

If a more realistic cast is desired, *all fins* can be cut from the wax cast body of the fish and replaced with fins carved out of Celluloid or other plastic-like material which is available in sheet form. Another method is to mold the fins and cast them in plastic (see Fins in the latter part of this chapter). In either method it is necessary to carve out holes in the wax body to receive the artificial fins. When producing the fins, leave enough material at their bases for anchoring within the wax body. Insert the fins, place in position, and anchor them from behind the wax cast with cotton and hot wax. Finish anchoring one fin before starting on another. An addition of wax will be necessary to the base of the fins at the show side of the fish. Do this carefully with a ¼- or ½-inch brush. Then model for correct anatomy by scraping or adding wax as needed. The areas where the fins were inserted can be made smooth by going over them with a piece of cloth which has been dipped in turpentine.

CASTS IN COMPOUND

Before plastics were developed commercially to a point where they could be poured or spread in a mold and set without oven treatment in high degrees of heat, I cast fish in a compound or composition material which proved satisfactory in producing fairly strong and durable mounts. The composition that is referred to as casting compound in this book is a mixture of asbestos, dextrin, whiting, glycerin, molding plaster, and a touch of carbolic acid. The formula and the directions for preparing this compound are found in Chapter 12. Casting in compound requires much more time than casting in plastics (next section), and it is more complicated. The materials which form the compound, however, are inexpensive in comparison to plastics.

The entire fish, including pectoral and ventral fins (if they are folded against the body while molding), can be cast in this pastelike medium. If the pectoral fin is to be extended away from the body, it can be cast in plastic or cut and carved out of a sheet of Celluloid. All the fins can be carved, if so desired, out of any type of sheet plastic-like material. The tail can be replaced also, but I advise against this because it is practically

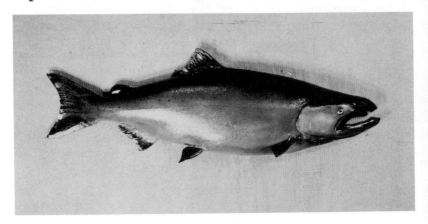

Fig. 49. King salmon produced in casting compound.

impossible to retain the natural contours of the body where it meets the tail.

Select the side of the mold which will reproduce the show side of the fish. Cut the oblong piece of plaster out of the other half of the mold, saw off the tail, and chip out the fin areas as described previously (Figs. 39 to 44). Shellac the mold (thinned 50–50 with alcohol) until a sheen is evident. Apply the wax-kerosene separator (formula No. 6 in Chapter 12).

Mix the casting compound with water and molding plaster. Trowel the first layer into both sides of the mold, to a depth of ⅛ inch. Then cut strips of cheesecloth that will fit conveniently into the cast—1 to 2 inches wide and about 4 to 8 inches in length, depending on the size of the fish. Press compound into these strips with a putty knife; use enough force so that the material is well impregnated. It is best to do this on a piece of glass that has been greased. Turn the strips over and apply them to the mold so that they meet or overlap each other a bit. Cover the entire area of both molds. Rub more compound over the cheesecloth layer after it has been placed in the mold before applying the next course. In small fishes two layers of material may be sufficient; however, as many layers as desired

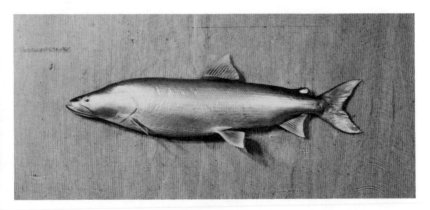

Fig. 50. Alaskan sheefish produced in casting compound.

may be worked into the cast. Allow one layer of reinforcement to set before placing the next one; otherwise, the cast will require an unnecessarily long time to dry. Be sure to add water and plaster to the casting compounds; it will facilitate setting of the compound. For certain purposes I have reinforced the cast with ⅛-inch mesh wire. Large fish can be strengthened with ¼-inch mesh wire. Cut the mesh wire into strips, place them lengthwise into the cast, and secure them with compound.

After the compound has set, trim the cast in both halves of the mold where the edge of the cast meets the edge of the shelf. Place the halves together and check to see that they fit snugly. If they don't, notice the spots which are responsible and trim away a bit more of the cast. When you are satisfied that the halves fit well, tie wire around each end of the mold so that the halves cannot be jarred from position. Now reach inside the cast and dampen, with a sponge and water, the area along the seams where the two halves of the cast meet. With a narrow spatula press compound (mixed with plaster and water) along the seams. Then cut a few narrow lengths (an inch or two wide depending on the size of the fish) of cheesecloth into which casting compound has been pressed. Insert these strips along the seams and bind them thoroughly to the cast with more compound.

Place the mold containing the cast over a radiator or in a warm room for faster drying. If the cast is not thoroughly dried when removing the mold, parts of the surface of the cast will remain in the mold and thus your fish will be ruined. To be certain no damage will occur to the show side, remove the back side of the mold first—when it is set and dry. The back side will usually be ready to come clear first. Then leave the fish in the show side of the mold for another day or two in the drying room—to make doubly sure that the cast is dried thoroughly. Then chip away, with a small hammer and chisel, around the edges of the mold holding the cast. This procedure will facilitate release of the cast from the mold.

If slight defects or air pockets appear in the cast, repair them with compound mixed liberally with plaster and water; or plaster alone mixed with water can be used.

Trim the body, fins, and tail and treat them lightly with fine sandpaper. It will be necessary to add casting compound along the outside of the seam where the two parts of the cast come together; allow to set, then trim and smooth with fine sandpaper.

Drill holes through the cast where the fins are to be located. Insert the bases of the artificial fins and secure them from the inside with the compound. It may be necessary to support the fins in position while the compound is setting. Modeling clay may be used for this purpose. Also, it may be wise not to place all the fins at one time. In other words, it is less awkward to

place a fin or two and wait until they have set in position before working on the others.

When the entire fish has dried thoroughly, apply a coat or
two of shellac (thinned 50–50 with alcohol) to every part of
the fish, including the back side.

Set the eye (see latter part of this chapter) and paint the fish
(Chapter 5). Apply a coat or two of clear varnish to every part
of the fish. If the fish is to be placed on a plaque, insert a block
of wood as described earlier.

CASTS IN PLASTICS
OR RESINS

The invention of durable, synthetic material which can be
cast in plaster molds, without requiring intense heat to set, has
been the most important contribution ever made to the art of
fish mounting. Other ways of making fish trophies, silhouettes,
plaster casts, skin mounts, etc., are fun; and I like to putter
with them myself, but the method which produces the best results by far is casting the fish in synthetic or plastic-like materials
(see formulas No. 1 and No. 2 and Plastics and Resins in Chapter 12).

Prepare the two-piece mold as described in the first part of
this chapter.

Applying Plastic

With a spatula apply formula No. 1. If this mixture has been
properly combined as directed, no excessive flowing of the
material should take place; that is, the material should, more or
less, stay where put (Fig. 53). Of course, the fin and tail areas
have to be covered also. Do not apply the casting mixture
above the edge of the impression of the fish; however, spread
it to include about ½ inch beyond the margins of the tail and
fins on the show side of the mold. Spread the material carefully in a thin layer over the entire impression of the fish. The

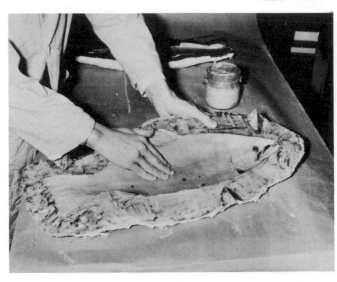

Fig. 51. The first step in casting in plastic is to apply the wax-kerosene separator.

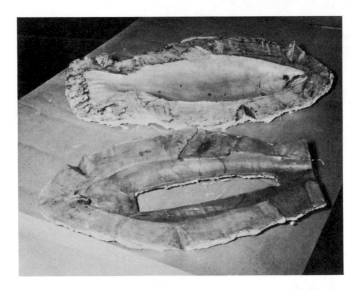

Fig. 52. Apply the separator to both halves of the mold.

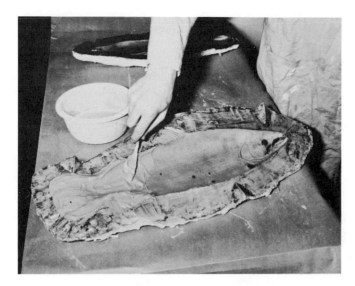

Fig. 53. Apply the plastic with a spatula.

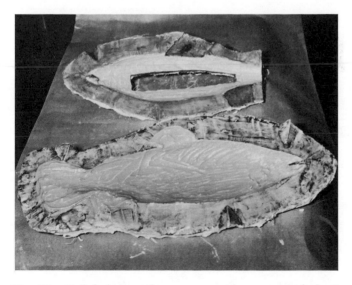

Fig. 54. Both halves as they appear with one coat of plastic.

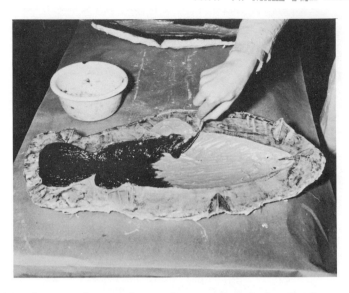

Fig. 55. The second or reinforcing layer is applied after the first coat of plastic has set. This mixture appears black in the photo because it has asbestos mixed in the formula No. 2.

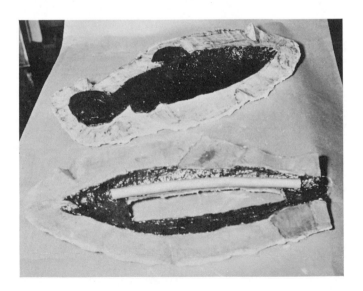

Fig. 56. Both sides are reinforced with this mixture. The wall side of the cast is reinforced also with a piece of conduit pipe as shown. The pipe is attached to the mold with plastic.

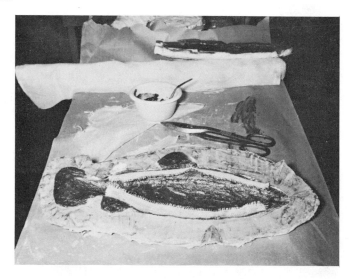

Fig. 57. When securing the halves of the cast together, in larger fish, place narrow strips of woven glass over the seam after the second application of plastic. The other half of the mold goes over this. More plastic is applied from the inside, along the strips of glass cloth—thus binding them to the cast.

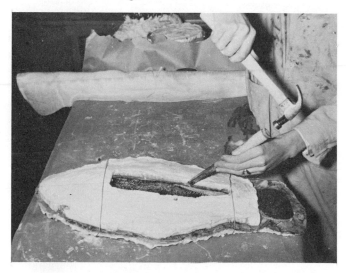

Fig. 58. The first step in removing the cast from the mold is to chip away any plastic which may have flowed over the edge of the back opening of the mold.

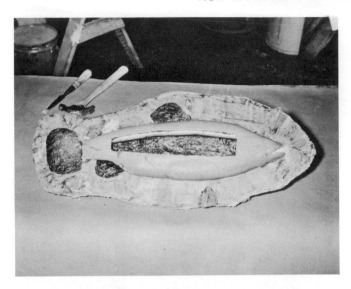

Fig. 59. Separate the halves of the mold by inserting a chisel between
them. The cast will remain in one side.

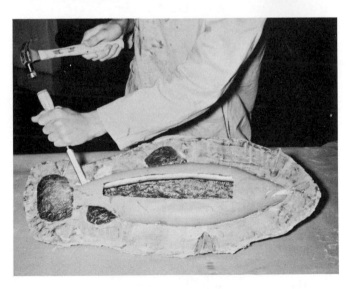

Fig. 60. Tap a chisel into the plaster about ¼ to ½ inch away from the
cast at the caudal peduncle.

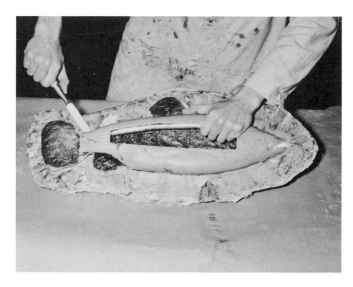

Fig. 61. Apply downward pressure on the chisel and the cast should come out.

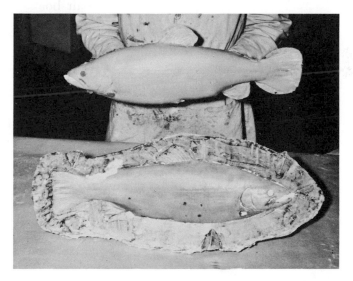

Fig. 62. The cast of the brown trout as it appears when removed from the mold.

other half of the mold (which will be the back side of the fish) does not require the application of the casting substance over the fin areas (obviously, they have been chipped away) because space is needed to accommodate the cast fins, which are thicker than the original fins, included in the other half of the mold.

Within a couple of hours the first coat should be set enough (even if not completely hard to the touch) to receive the second or reinforcing layer (Fig. 55). Formula No. 2 for this layer, which has more body to it, will be found in Chapter 12. Apply it in the same manner as the first coat.

If you are using other material as the casting medium—such as resins which are used with Fiberglas to repair boat hulls—the same techniques of application are employed.

Strengthening the Cast

Medium size fishes—specimens between 10 and 20 pounds—require stronger casts. This is accomplished by backing the first layer of plastic in the mold with glass cloth or woven glass (Fig. 63) and additional plastic.

When the first plastic layer of the cast has set hard, a glossy surface will appear. Dull it with sandpaper so that the next layer of plastic will stick to it better. Now cut the glass cloth with tin snips so as to line the cast inside the mold, snugly. The glass cloth is fitted easier if it is cut in sections. Remove the woven glass and spread formula No. 1 over the inside of the cast. Then again place the cloth in position in the cast and spread formula No. 1 over it. Apply some pressure to the spatula so that the plastic will be forced through the weave and thus bind with the plastic underneath. The initial coat of plastic has to be completed in one operation, but the application of woven glass and plastic is accomplished easier and better if it is done in sections.

Big-game fishes such as marlin and tuna may be reinforced with two layers of glass cloth and plastic, and further with pieces of thin-wall conduit (Figs. 65 and 66) or any similar type of pipe. I use conduit because it is light in weight, not ex-

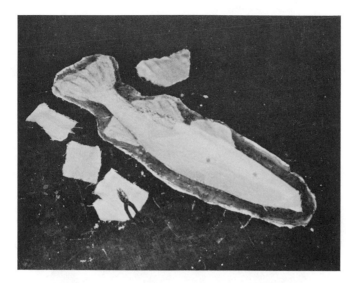

Fig. 63. Medium and large fishes require stronger casts. This is accomplished by backing the first layer of plastic in the mold with glass (woven glass) and an additional layer of plastic.

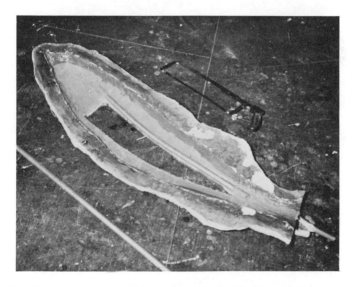

Fig. 64. Conduit pipe should be secured to both sides of the opening of the wall side of a large fish.

pensive, easy to cut and bend, and strong for the purpose. Cut
the conduit with a hack saw and bend it into shape in a vise.
The pipe should fit as closely as possible into the contours of
the cast. When all the required pieces are placed in position,
bind them permanently to the cast with pieces of woven glass
and plastic. The conduit will not only reinforce the hollow

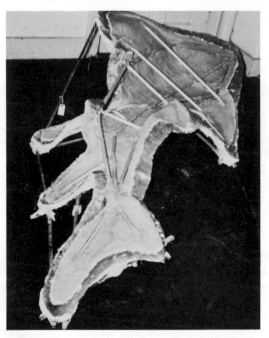

Fig. 65. The cast of a shovelnose ray in the mold. A large fish such as
this should be strengthened with conduit pipe while the cast is in the
mold.

mold but will supply an attachment for hanging the mount on
the wall.

When the plastic material has set, chip away any bits of
plastic that may extend beyond the edges of the fish impression
of the mold. Now place the halves together and see if they fit
snugly. If they do not, it will be necessary to file or chip away
the small areas of plastic, from the edges of the cast, which
prevent complete contact of the halves of the mold. The

chipped away areas in the back half of the mold, which accommodate the cast fins of the fish, may need additional chipping if there are any irregularities that hinder a good fit of the two sides of the mold (Figs. 42 and 43).

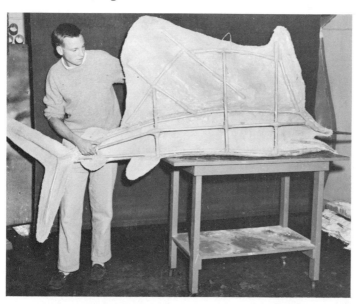

Fig. 66. John Carmody, Yale student, holds a cast of a Pacific sailfish so that the reinforcing structure can be shown.

Securing the Halves

Wire the ends of the mold so that they cannot be moved out of position. With a narrow spatula spread the plastic mixture, (formula No. 2 in Chapter 12) along the seams inside the cast where the two halves meet. One application is sufficient to bind the two sections of cast together strongly. In a fish longer than about 30 inches, however, it is a good idea to place narrow strips of woven glass cloth over the seams after the second application of plastic and then spread more plastic over the glass cloth (Fig. 57).

Before putting the halves together, I like to attach a piece of thin-wall conduit along the upper edge of the back side of the cast, although it is not absolutely necessary (Fig. 56). The conduit, which is secured to the cast with plastic, makes a nice, smooth, strong edge for handling the cast. Also, it makes hanging the fish very easy. (See Conduit Pipe in Chapter 12.)

Removing Cast from Mold

Several hours are required for the cast to set hard. To remove the cast from a two-piece mold, first chip away any plastic which may have flowed over the edge of the back opening of the mold (Fig. 58). Tap a chisel between the halves, here and there, until the mold separates. Usually, a bit of jiggling with the chisel at the tail end of the mold will release the back side of the mold first. The whole fish now remains in the show side of the mold. Tap a chisel into the plaster about ¼ to ½ inch inch away from the cast at the caudal peduncle (Figs. 60 and 61). Then apply pressure to the chisel as you force it down. If there are no outstanding undercuts in the mold, the cast should be relieved without complication. If the cast does not release easily, however, proceed to chip away the edge of the mold where it meets the cast. Use care so that the chisel does not damage the cast. Often the troublesome undercuts will be found in the mold in the area of the fish's lower jaw. Return to the caudal peduncle, insert the chisel again, and this time the cast should come away easily.

Cleaning and Finishing the Cast

Usually, in the process of casting, some of the separator wax will be transferred from the mold to the cast. With a cloth dipped in turpentine, rub the affected area until the wax on the cast is lost. Wash the entire cast with a household abrasive cleanser and very hot water. Use a stiff scrub brush. File the edges of the opening in the back side of the cast until smooth.

With a fine-tooth jig saw (a metal cutting blade is best), cut the excess material from around the mouth, fins, and tail. Mark the outline of the fins with a soft pencil so that they can be followed easier with the saw (Figs. 67 and 68). Do not make

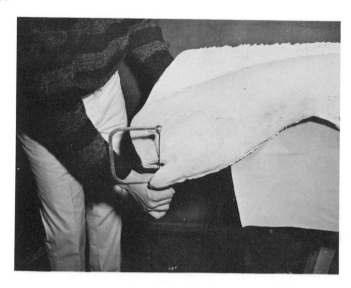

Fig. 67. In open mouth casts, where a mold and cast of the mouth have been made separately (Figs. 22 and 78), the plastic across the opening of the mouth has to be sawed out. A fine-tooth blade for cutting metal is best.

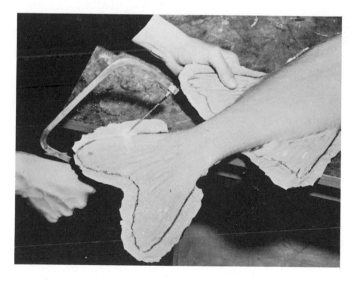

Fig. 68. Cut the excess material from around the fins.

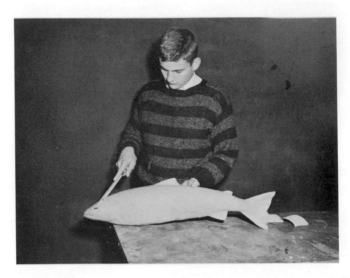

Fig. 69. Pete Dietrich, Yale student, files and sands the seam of the cast where the halves have been joined together.

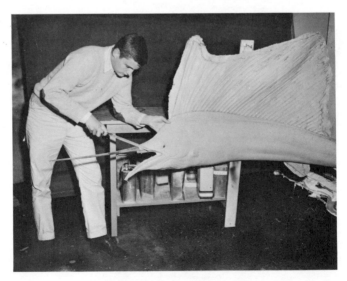

Fig. 70. If the original bill of a sailfish or marlin is used, file and sand the area where the bill has been joined to the cast.

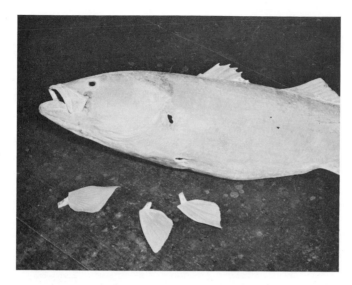

Fig. 71. The areas which accommodate the bases of the pectoral and ventral fins have been drilled out.

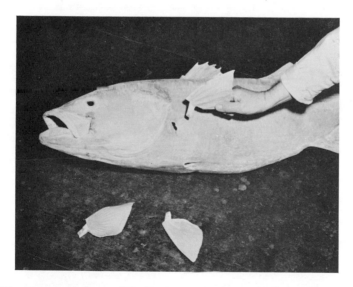

Fig. 72. Notice the base of the fin which is shaped to fit the hole. Place plastic around the edges of the hole and also around the base of the fin. Then prop the fin in position until the plastic has hardened.

the ends of the fin rays too smooth; cut into them a bit in order to produce a more effective, natural appearance.

Use a file to go over the seam where the halves of the cast come together (Fig. 69). It may be necessary to add plastic to the crevices in the seam. A heavy mix of molding plaster and water may be used instead of plastic. Also, use plaster to fill in all the pin holes and to repair any other imperfections in the cast. Another method is to use silver paste and liquid that is standard for painting radiators. Mix just enough liquid with the paste to facilitate its application over the cast by rubbing with the fingers. In this manner all the tiny defects will be filled in. File and sand the areas repaired in plastic. With a pointed tool or small fine file accentuate any lines in the cast necessary; lines between the jaws, end of the gill cover, nostrils, etc.

With a drill, cut through the cast in the area where the base of the pectoral and ventral fins will be located (Fig. 71). Also, drill out material from the spot which is to receive the artificial eye. Make the hollow large enough to accommodate the glass eye with room to spare because a substance such as plastic or wax has to be inserted first to hold the eye.

Fins

If the fins have been preserved and as yet not molded, see *Molding the Fins* in Chapter 2. When the molds of the fins are dried, chisel or dig out the plaster adjacent to the base of the fins on both sides of the mold (Figs. 26 and 28). In this way provision is made for an extension at the base of the cast fin for use when attaching the fins to the body. Shellac and apply separator (same as body mold) before casting.

To cast the fins (Figs. 73 to 76), use formula No. 1 (do not include asbestos) found in Chapter 12. Spread the substance into both halves of the mold and cover only the impression of the fins. Now place the halves together and apply steady pressure so that the mold halves slowly come together (Fig. 75). Do not press so strongly that no space remains between the halves. On the other hand, do not leave too much width be-

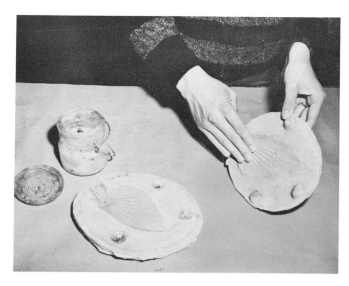

Fig. 73. The first step in casting the fins is to apply the wax-kerosene separator. Rub it well into the mold with your fingers.

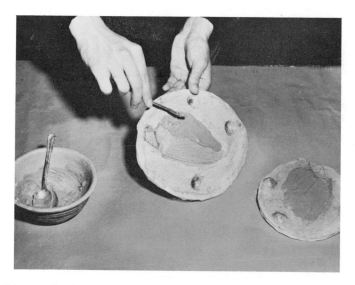

Fig. 74. Apply the plastic to both halves of the mold—formula No. 1.

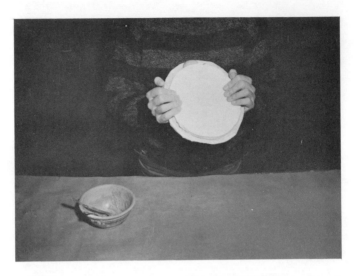

Fig. 75. Employ steady pressure so that the mold halves come together slowly.

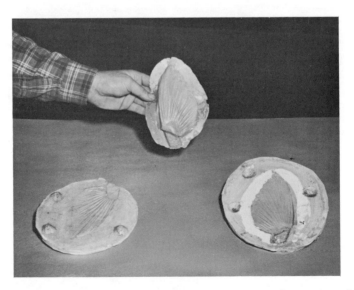

Fig. 76. A pectoral fin of a striped bass as it appears when removed from the mold.

tween the halves because the fins will be too thick and therefore appear artificial. Do not apply an excessive amount of plastic or you will have to keep wiping the sides of the mold, and this makes a messy job.

When the plastic has set, tap a chisel here and there between the halves of the mold until they separate. If difficulty is encountered in taking apart the mold, it is an indication that the separator was too thin or did not entirely cover the mold surface. Both sides of the mold will never release from the cast fin simultaneously. When one half is removed, the other half will still hold the cast fin. Therefore, it is necessary to insert a chisel gently around the cast in order to pry it away from the mold. Immersion of the mold and cast in hot water, or application of heat, will soften the cast fin so that its removal can be accomplished without breaking.

Clean the casts, wipe off any separator wax with a cloth dipped in turpentine, and wash them well in soap and warm water. Then outline the fins with a pencil and cut them out with a jig saw. Be sure an extension of the base of the fin remains. Before placing the fins, make sure that you secure a lifelike curvature. This applies to the tail and the fins on the main cast as well as to those that have been cast separately. Let hot water run over them until they become pliable (the pectoral and ventral fins can be held in a small pail of hot water). As you remove them from the hot water, shape them quickly and hold them in position with finger pressure until cool. When cool they again become rigid but remain in their new shape. The fins can be heated and reshaped any number of times. I use cloth-lined rubber gloves so that my fingers will not get burned. Under no circumstances attempt to curve the fins when they are not thoroughly heated and pliable, or they will crack.

Now place the pectoral and ventral fins. If they don't fit into their respective holes easily, file away more of the area. Mix a small batch of formula No. 2, place some around the base of the fins, and insert them. A support is necessary to hold the fins in position until the plastic at their bases has set hard.

Some additional application of plastic will be necessary to bring the base of the fins to their former contours. Use a small file carefully and follow with fine sandpaper in order to remove any rough spots.

Mouth

If you have made a separate mold of the mouth, prepare it like any other for casting: allow to dry, shellac, and rub on separator. It is best to make the cast in two pieces. Do one side, wait till it hardens, apply the separator to the edges, and then apply the plastic to the other side. After these two pieces have been removed from the mold, they are clinched together with fresh plastic where they meet at the rear of the mouth (Fig. 78). A one-piece cast can be made around the mold, but then it is a chore to dig out the goodly amount of plaster which is in the mold. The plaster cannot be removed in a single solid form because of the numerous angles and undercuts in the mold.

Trim the cast of the mouth so that it fits accurately into the jaws of the fish, then secure it in place with plastic. It is best to do this from the inside. After this plastic has set hard, fill in the seam where the mouth meets the jaws with additional plastic.

Eye

Paint the glass eye (see Chapter 5). Protect the paint from contact with the plastic, if plastic is used to set the eye in place, by dropping hot wax over the painted side of the eye. If wax is used to set the eye, place the glass eye snugly into the socket while the wax is still soft.

Bills or Spears

The mold of a sailfish, marlin, or swordfish can be made to include the bill or spear. When the cast is built the bill will also be reproduced in the artificial medium. It is possible, how-

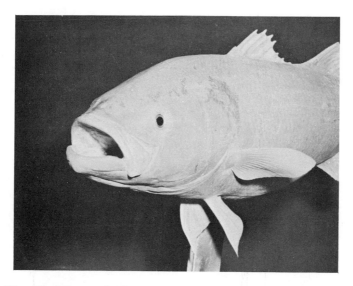

Fig. 77.   The plastic which covered the mouth has been cut away. Notice
the flowing curves which have been formed into the fins.

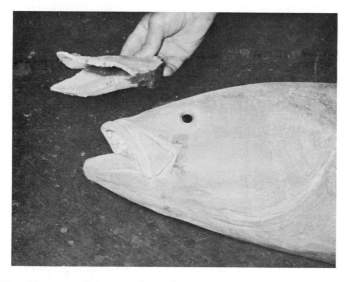

Fig. 78.   The cast of the mouth ready to be inserted—usually through the
inside of the head.

ever, to use the original bill in the mount. Prepare the bill as described in Chapter 8. When applying plastic for the cast, place the bill in position and trowel plastic into the base of the bill and the head of the mount or cast. Reinforce the connection with heavy annealed wire, woven glass cloth, and more plastic. Smooth the connection with a file and sand paper (Fig. 70).

4

Skinning and Skin Mounts

Throughout this book I state repeatedly that for a really lifelike trophy the fish should be molded and cast without trying to preserve the original skin. But some anglers may want to try their hands at a skin mount. And there are sometimes occasions when it is not possible to bring a whole specimen safely home but when the skin can easily be removed and transported (see Chapter 1). So every angler should be interested in the proper way to skin a fish. He should also know something about how to mount a skin as a trophy—if only to be able to judge some of the misshapen horrors he will see in museums and elsewhere!

SKINNING THE FISH

If the specimen is fresh, remove the slime as described in Chapter 2. If the fish is frozen, thaw it out. Be sure the fins and tail are soft; if they are dried and brittle, damage may occur during the skinning. With a piece of wet cotton dab the fins and tail occasionally to keep them from drying.

A Formalin specimen should be soaked in several changes of fresh water over a day or two and then dunked in a solution of sodium bisulfite and sodium sulfite (see formula No. 3 in Chapter 12) so that the pungent odor of the Formalin will be eliminated. Also, during the skinning process the fish should be rinsed frequently in fresh water. I advise the use of rubber gloves in skinning a fish which has been preserved in Formalin. The skinner's eyes may smart a bit if the fish is not soaked enough in clean water. There is an advantage to Formalin-preserved specimens because the skin *will never* stretch out of shape during skinning.

The skin, fins, and tail must be kept moist during the process of skinning or else scales will be lost and fins will crack. I prefer to keep the fish on water-soaked cloths while working. Select the show side of the fish and then turn it over; obviously, the cut has to be made on the opposite side. For the initial incision run the knife or scalpel along the mid-side of the body from the edge of the gill cover to the tail fin (Fig. 79).

Lift the gill cover, insert the scissors into the incision, and point toward the head. Cut through the bony structure which is the piece of anatomy on which the rear edge of the gill cover naturally rests. This step may be done later as indicated in Fig. 84.

Separate the skin from the body along the incision (Fig. 80). Push the knife here and there; use your fingers and thumb as much as possible in the process. Some types of fish skin, however have to be cut from the body during the entire process of skinning; the skin cannot be pulled away with the fingers. Care should be used not to cut through the skin. If it is damaged do not panic; it can be repaired in the finished mount. Do not give rough treatment to any fish skin. A mount with many missing scales is not very attractive.

Continue separating the skin from the body until the pectoral fin is reached; snip it at its base. As the skinning proceeds to the other fins, cut them from the body also (Fig. 82). Exercise caution here because it is easy to insert the tips of the scissors too far and damage the skin. Often, skinning may be facilitated by slicing through and removing a segment of the body (Fig. 81). Carefully skin down to the tail and cut through the body about an inch or two away from the base of the tail. Now, cut through the body close to the head and snip the backbone with a strong pair of scissors. I prefer to use a pair of tin snips.

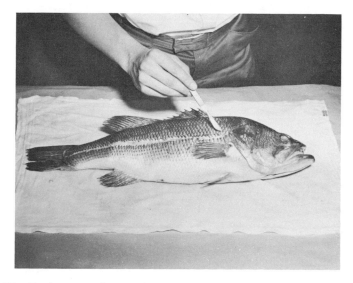

Fig. 79. In skinning, the initial incision is made by running a scalpel along the mid-side of the body from the edge of the gill cover to the tail fin.

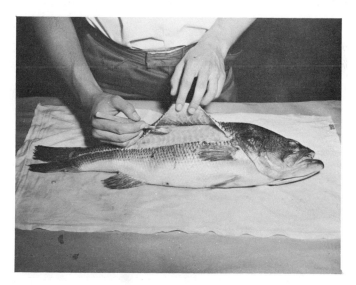

Fig. 80. Separate the skin from the body along the incision.

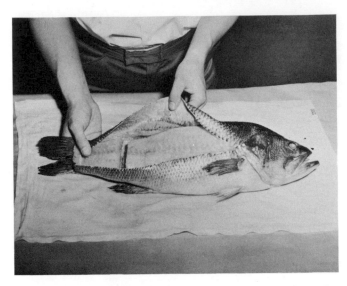

Fig. 81. Often, skinning may be facilitated by slicing through and removing a segment of body.

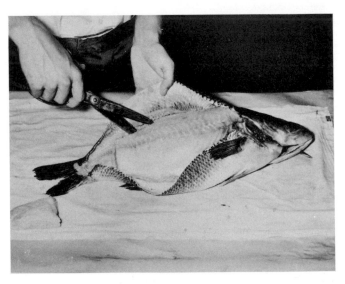

Fig. 82. As the skinning proceeds, cut the fins from the body on the
inside.

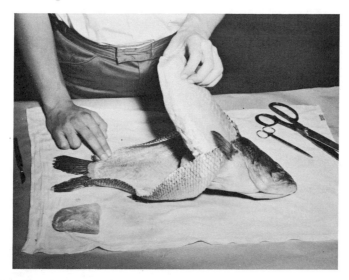

Fig. 83. Continue skinning until the body is free up to the head.

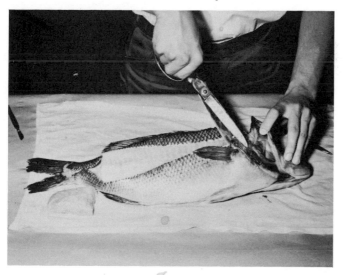

Fig. 84. Cut through the bony structure, the piece of anatomy on which the rear edge of the gill cover naturally rests. This step may be done at any time during the process of skinning.

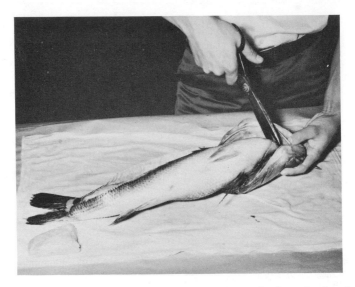

Fig. 85.   Cut the throat skin where it is attached to the head.

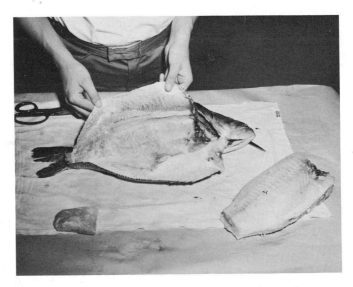

Fig. 86.   The skin as it appears with the body removed.

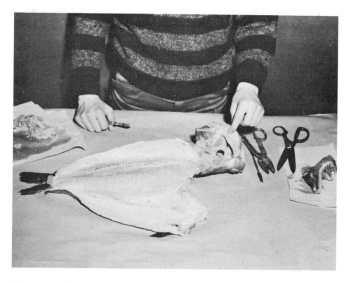

Fig. 87. Snip the gills at their extremities and remove them entirely.

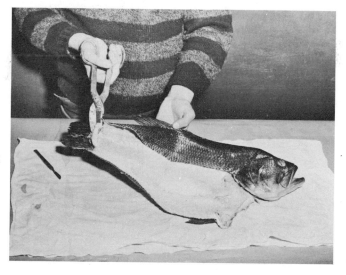

Fig. 88. Skin the tail to the base of the rays and remove the inch or two of tail which remains. Go over the entire skin and scrape away all bits of flesh.

Bend the head down and finish separating it from the body. Continue skinning until the entire body is free. Dispose of the body. Cut the throat skin where it meets the head as indicated in Fig. 85. It is possible, but more difficult, to skin out the flesh in this area while leaving the skin attached to the head.

Return to the head; snip the gills at their extremities and remove them entirely (Fig. 87). Some taxidermists recommend leaving the gills within the head. Why, I don't know. The less flesh, bone, and tissue remaining in the skin the better the mount will be. Remove as much flesh and bone from the head as possible. Gouge out the eyes. Cut into the cheeks from the inside and scrape out all the meat; cut the tongue at its base and remove. Cut into the skull—of course from the inside— many times with heavy shears or scissors and gouge away as much of the bony structure as possible. If small pieces of the head skin are damaged, they can be repaired in the mounted fish. Return to the base of the fins and cut and scrape away all the flesh clinging to the base of the spines. Then skin the tail to the base of the rays and remove the inch or two of body which remains (Fig. 88). Go over the entire fish and carefully scrape away all bits of flesh from the skin.

Skinning can be interrupted at any time after the body is removed for almost any period of time if the skin is placed in a saturated salt solution. Simply fill a pan with water and add salt until it will no longer disappear. Be sure no part of the fish skin remains out of the water.

Preserving the Skin

If the skin is greasy, wipe it thoroughly and soak it in water containing a strong detergent. There are many good household soap fluids on the market today; or you can use a strong brown soap. I do not recommend that the amateur use gasoline or carbon tetrachloride to remove grease because it is too dangerous. If an adult angler feels he must use gasoline as a grease remover, he should do it outdoors a good distance from home. Under no circumstances should young boys use it.

Many taxidermists and teachers of taxidermy advocate painting the inside of a fish skin with an arsenic paste or fluid preparation; this is ridiculous. Arsenic is a poison that should not be used by *amateurs* in fish mounting or in any other form of taxidermy for that matter. Bugs cannot get into a properly mounted fish skin that has been varnished or lacquered, and that is the purpose of using arensic—to keep the bugs from eating the specimen!

If the fish is well cleaned the only preservative the skin requires (if it has not been in Formalin) is salt; rub it well into every part of the skin. Roll the skin up and leave it overnight. A better method is to cover the skin with salt, place it in a can, and add just enough water to cover the skin. Let it soak for a day or so. The salt will draw out juices in the skin. Be sure to rinse out all salt before mounting the skin.

A 10 per cent solution of Formalin—nine parts water, one part Formalin—is a powerful disinfectant and a highly efficient preservative. The skin and bits of flesh inside the head can be preserved better by applying the Formalin with a brush. Do not apply this liquid, however, until the skin is placed in the mold or ready for mounting because the Formalin will set the skin in short order in whatever position it happens to be at the timo of application of Formalin. Be sure to read Formalin in Chapter 12.

I feel strongly against using materials such as gasoline and arsenic on fish skins because there is no necessity for employing such dangerous items. My first attempt at fish preservation was at the age of five when I preserved two cunners, partially skinned and housed in a jar of salt and water. I kept this trophy on a small table by my bed for a couple of years until the salt ate through the metal cover of the jar! At the age of seven I caught my first trout which was a gigantic 14 inches in length. I was beside myself with concern when I realized that my great trophy would not last forever in the ice box. With tears in my eyes I cut off the brown trout's tail and then skinned one side of the fish—minus head and fins. I scraped the inside of the skin with my penknife. I glued the skin on a neat piece of cardboard and the tail on another. Many years have passed since that memorable day, but I still display the skin and tail of that brown trout as one of the most cherished possessions in my tackle room.

My first whole fish mount was a yellow perch that was skinned and stuffed with plaster. I filled the eye socket with plaster and painted in a black pupil. Then I varnished the fish and screwed a backboard to it. I mounted that perch at the age of nine. The point I am trying to make is that the trout skin and the perch were not treated with gasoline or arsenic or any type of preservative, and yet they appear to be in the same condition today as they were many years ago.

In the field, when conservation of time is important, it is not necessary to do a thorough job. The body of the fish must be removed from the skin—a job that does not require much time. Also, snip out the gills and eyes. But the head need not be cleaned, and the fine work of removing flesh from the skin and base of fins need not be carried out. However, be sure to do a thorough job of salting.

SKIN MOUNTS

Mounted Skins

One of the easiest methods of preserving a fish skin for display is to mount the skin of only one complete side. Clean the slime from the fish and remove the skin from the body. Then, with a sharp knife or scissors cut the skin along the median line of the back and belly. Of course, leave the tail and fins on the side of the skin which is to be preserved. Only one of the abdominal or ventral fins will be kept because the skin is cut down the middle of the belly. After cleaning and wiping away as much of the moisture as possible, the skin is brushed with glue (ten parts glue to one part glycerin) and placed on the intended plaque or backboard. Place wax paper over the skin, add layers of newspaper over it, and apply some weight over all.

After the fish skin is thoroughly dry, paint it and give the skin and backboard a coat of varnish. An attractive collection of trophies can be produced very easily in this manner. Information on the weight of the fish, and when and where caught, can be entered on each plaque to add interest to the collection.

Excelsior Body

The most primitive method of fish mounting, which is still practiced, is the placement of the skin over an artificial body or mannequin. The worst type of body for mounting is produced by the use of excelsior and thread over a core of wood. The artificial body must be in the shape of the original but slightly smaller. Then a thin coat of clay, papier-mâché, varnish, or other type of coating is placed over the mannequin so that it becomes smooth and will not absorb moisture. Papier-mâché is stuffed into the head, and the skin is draped around the artificial body. Incidentally, forget about papier-mâché; it is an outmoded material. The excelsior body method of mounting a fish is hopeless; do not use it.

Wood Mannequin

This method is an improvement over the excelsior body. Any angler handy with carpenter tools may find it interesting. Outline the fish on paper and then transfer the outline onto a block of wood at least as wide as the body of the fish. A few pieces of wood may have to be glued together. Choose soft wood such as white pine, which is easy to work. Cut out the fish along the outline. If a band saw is not available, use any saw and finish the job with a wood rasp. Now, with cutting tools and rasps proceed to produce a wooden body which resembles the original body of the fish as closely as possible—all measurements must be exact. The wooden form should fit into the head of the fish but not tightly—leave some room for casting compound. If the mount is to have an open mouth, cut the wood accordingly. Rough sandpaper the wooden body and then follow with fine sandpaper. The body must be without flaws and absolutely smooth. Apply a couple of coats of shellac to the body, and it is now ready to receive the skin.

Process the skin as described previously. Brush a thin coat of carpenter's glue and glycerin (see Chapter 12) around the wooden form. Push some casting compound into the bases of the tail and fins, and then place the skin around the form. Tack the skin along the incision on the back side. Now, force some compound into the head and through the mouth and gill opening; build out the cheeks, eye socket, jaws, etc. If the mount has an open mouth, place more of the compound inside and model it directly as the compound begins to set.

Model the compound into place around the base of the tail and fins by pressing and pushing the material here and there from the outside with thumb and fingers. The fins and tail are soft and pliable but will set in a shrivelled and awkward position unless supported until dried with stiff paper and clips (Fig. 101). Do not pull the fins away from the body. After the fish has dried—the time depends upon weather or amount of heat in a room—clean out the eye socket, add some casting compound or hot wax, and insert the glass eye (see Chapter 5). If the specimen is thoroughly dry, shrinkage will appear about the head—cheeks, lips, jaws, etc. It is not necessary, but if the angler desires a better mount, the head should be reconstructed to its former full contours by brushing on melted wax. If the scales show a tendency to lift, brush a thin coat of glue over them.

Shellac the entire fish. Thin down the shellac with alcohol so that it will flow on easily and not leave brush marks. Screw a piece of wood temporarily onto the back of the fish to support it while painting (see Chapter 5). The best approach is to select a piece of wood 3 or 4 inches wide and about a foot and a half in length. With the fish attached to it, the upright can be placed in a vise and moved up or down to the most comfortable height for painting. Finish the wooden plaque before attaching the fish to it. A screw eye may be inserted into the back of the fish instead for hanging on the wall.

This method of fish mounting is far from the best; however, anyone handy with tools will find it fun. And with care a pleasingly presentable mount can be achieved. Twenty-two years ago the first taxidermy job for which I received payment was a 16-inch rainbow trout. I put my heart and soul into the mount which was done by the above method. The mount still looks presentable. I have tried to buy it back from Dr. Joseph DeVita, a veterinarian, for whom I did the job. I would love to have it in my tackle room as a memento. However, he attaches as much sentimental value to it as I would. The rainbow remains displayed proudly in his office and he will not sell! I did manage to photograph it, however, as Fig. 89.

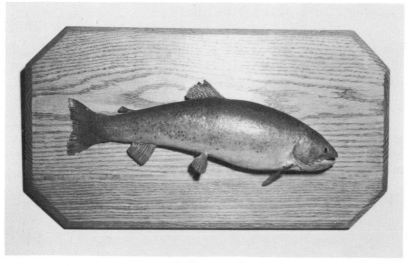

Fig. 89. This rainbow, a skin over a wooden body, was mounted by the author twenty-two years ago. It has never needed repair and is in surprisingly good condition.

Skin Mounts—Half Mold

One of the easiest ways to mount a fish is to use a one-side mold as a guide or form to fill out the skin with molding plaster or casting compound. A mold for this purpose does not have to be clear in scale definition, nor have a smooth shelf, nor do the fins have to be included in the mold. This method requires less time than any other in molding.

Construct a wooden box big enough to allow 4 or 5 inches of room on all sides of the fish. The sides need not be more than a few inches high (Fig. 90). Place a piece of newspaper inside this receptacle to act as a separator between the plaster and the wood. Pour the plaster directly into the box. Then place the fish gently on the soft plaster and press it in slowly until the mid-line of the back and belly is reached. The underside of the fins and tail now are in contact with the plaster. Before the plaster has thoroughly set, dig away some of it from around the ventral fins so that they are not buried. When the plaster has set, remove the fish and skin it.

Now place the skin in the mold. Check carefully so that every portion of the skin fits accurately into the mold. If you wish to brush a 10 per cent solution of Formalin on the inside of the skin, head, and body, now is the time to do it.

Fill the downside of the body with plaster or casting compound. If plaster is used, it should be mixed to a heavier consistency than for molding—like whipped cream. Spoon it into the head; press well forward to be sure it fills all parts. Work smartly; the plaster has to be of the proper consistency to push around, but that is only a step away from setting. Place a piece of looped wire into the back of the plaster. Turn the ends so that the wire cannot pull out. This will serve well for hanging the fish on the wall. A piece of skin may have to be cut to accommodate the wire. Obviously, the wire should be shaped and ready before the plaster is mixed. Sew the skin together after the plaster has set in the body.

If the fish is intended to be attached to a wooden plaque, insert a piece of wood into the plaster while it is still soft (Fig. 98). The wood should be waterproofed by dipping it in hot paraffin wax. It can also be made moisture resistant by lacquering, painting, or by some other method. Here again it is obvious that the wood has to be prepared before attempting to mix the plaster. The plaque is attached to this piece of wood with a

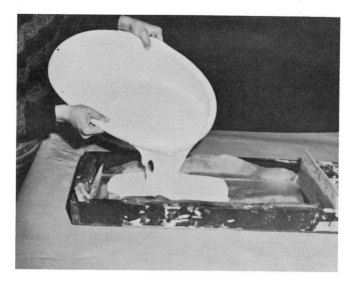

Fig. 90. Pour the plaster into a boxlike receptacle.

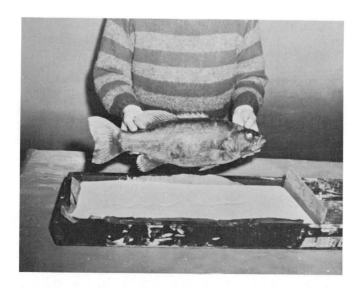

Fig. 91. Choose the show side of the smallmouth bass. This is the side that will go into the plaster.

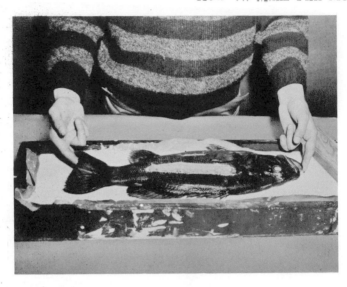

Fig. 92. Set the fish gently into the plaster so that exactly half the body
has sunk into the plaster.

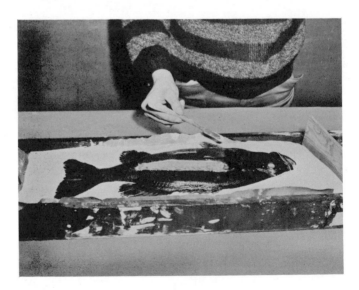

Fig. 93. When the plaster begins to set, dig it out from around the paired
ventral fins so that they will be free.

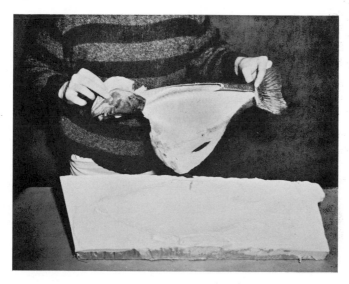

Fig. 94. Place the skin in the mold. Check carefully so that every portion
of the skin fits accurately.

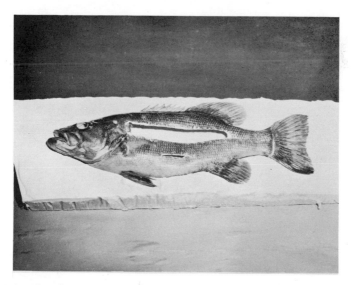

Fig. 95. The skin is now ready to receive the plaster (casting compound
mixed with water and plaster can be used instead of plaster).

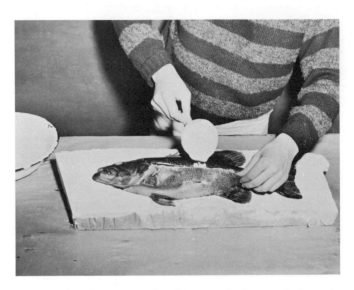

Fig. 96. Pour the plaster into the skin to a thickness of about ½ to ¾ of an inch.

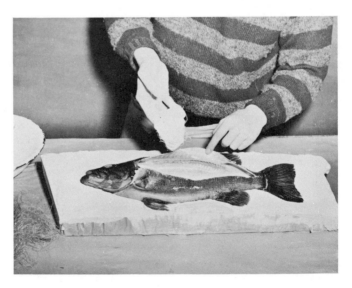

Fig. 97. Reinforce with sisal dipped in plaster.

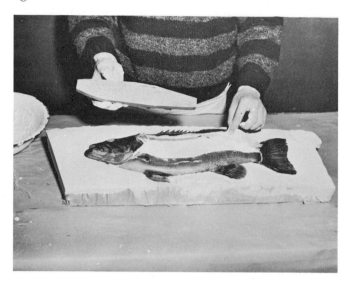

Fig. 98. Here you can insert a piece of wood, which has been water-proofed with lacquer or hot wax, directly into the plaster. The wood will serve as a base for attaching screw eyes or hanging wire, or a backboard can be screwed to it. A wire for hanging can be inserted into the plaster instead (while the plaster is still soft).

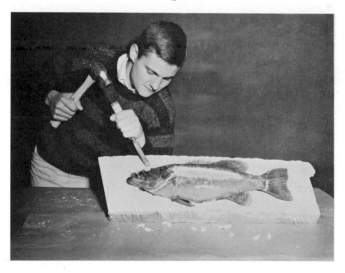

Fig. 99. It is better to chip away a bit of the mold so that the mount will release easily rather than to force the fish out of it.

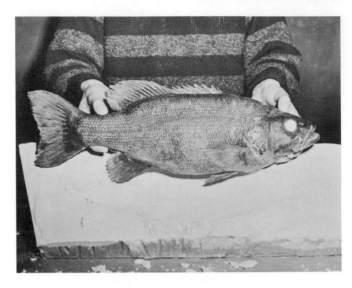

Fig. 100. The smallmouth bass as it appears when removed from the half mold.

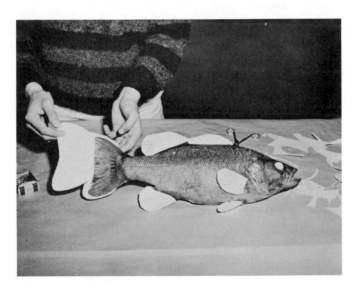

Fig. 101. Cut stiff paper or thin cardboard to the shape of the fins. With paper clips secure the two pieces to each fin until it dries into shape.

couple of screws. Drill holes in the plaque which will allow the screws to be dropped in freely up to their heads. Drill holes of a smaller diameter into the wood in the fish, which will accommodate the screws. If holes are not drilled, the wood may crack; or fins may be damaged due to the craftsman's struggle with the screw driver. Of course, the plaque should be stained and varnished before attaching the mounted fish to it. During the entire process the fins and tail should be kept moist so that they will not dry and crack.

Casting compound can be substituted for plaster in the same method (a one-sided mold). Using compound has an advantage because it can be mixed to a putty-like consistency and may be either troweled into the fish or worked with the fingers. Also, there is no urgency to work fast because compound mixed with plaster and water requires much more time to set.

Fill the head and line the body with about a ½-inch layer of compound. Insert the waterproofed wood block. I would recommend a piece of wood that is the shape of the body of the fish only smaller. The head end of the wood should be cut down so that plenty of room remains for compound. Place enough of the compound around the sides of the wood to fill out the skin to its former shape. Tack the skin to the block of wood after the compound has hardened. Care for the fins and finish the fish as described previously.

Whether using plaster or compound it is advantageous, although not necessary, to preserve the fish in Formalin (nine parts water, one part Formalin) for four or five hours so that the skin becomes rigid before molding the fish. For this purpose the fish need not be injected wih Formalin.

Skin Mounts—Full Mold

For the most lifelike results in skin mounts, I recommend the following method. Preserve the fish in Formalin (see Chapter 1), taking care that it is properly posed. A fish the size of a 16-inch trout or bass will require a few hours or an overnight immersion to harden the skin into shape. When ready for molding, remove the fish from the Formalin and let it soak in fresh water for a few hours. Change the water a couple of times.

Before starting to mold the fish, place a good wad of clay around the pectoral and ventral fins. Disregard the wall side pectoral fin. Shape enough of the clay around the fins so that the ends will protrude through the plaster. In other words, there will be holes in the mold. Wet strips of newspaper will do in a pinch. (Did you know that if newspaper is torn with the grain, long smooth-edged strips are obtained, while against the grain the strips are short and ragged edged?) This procedure will leave large enough holes in the mold to allow a place for the fins when filling the skin with compound.

Make a two-piece mold. Separate the halves, remove the fish, and place it in water so that the skin and fins will not shrivel. After the mold dries, saw out a slab of plaster lengthwise, about 2 inches wide in a mold of a 16-inch fish. Of course, the mold half which has taken the impression of the backside of the fish is the one to cut (Figs. 39 to 41). Dig out the clay which was placed around the fins before molding. It is best to continue the holes right through the mold if plaster has entirely covered the clay.

Skin the fish, rinsing it in water whenever the Formalin becomes irritating. Cut a piece of skin out of the backside of the fish about the same size and shape as the piece of plaster sawed out of the mold (Fig. 95). Wipe all excess moisture from the skin and place it on a flat surface; fill the head and trowel casting compound onto the inside of the skin to about ½ inch. Pour beach sand or some other dry grainy material into the fish. Place the two flaps of skins back to their original position. Now insert the fish carefully into the show side of the mold; insert the pectoral and ventral fins into their respective holes. Work the other half of the mold into position; be careful not to crease the skin of the fish between the edges of the mold. The skin may require trimming to coincide with the opening in the backside of the mold. Bind a piece of wire around each end of the mold so that the two pieces will stay snug. With the fingers press and push the sand around gently against the skin. Pour in more sand. Continue to work along until the fish will not accommodate any more sand.

The next day let the sand run out of the mold by turning it over. Do not, as yet, separate the mold halves. Set it aside to dry in a warm room or outdoors. Gradual drying is best. After a couple of days check the compound; if it has hardened, remove the specimen from the mold and store it in a safe place until thoroughly dry. If the fins or tail need to be shaped, relax them by tying water-soaked cotton around each. Then treat the fins as described earlier in this chapter.

Before painting the specimen it is best to wait until the fish dries—a couple of weeks or more, depending on drying conditions. If the head shrinks noticeably, return it to its former full contours by applying hot beeswax and modeling into shape. A mount of this type looks best without a plaque or backboard. If one is desired, however, clinch a piece of wood inside the fish with cotton and anchor permanently by applying hot wax over the cotton. The backboard can then be screwed to the wood which is inside the fish.

5

Painting the Mount

There are numerous ways of painting a trophy so that it will look attractive. The various methods include a wide range of techniques. In other words, there is a method that can be satisfactory for every degree of interest or ability, from a single application of one color for a silhouette effect to the exacting reproduction of the true coloration of live fishes which can be accomplished only by a skilled artist.

Preparing the Surface

For painting, the mount first requires a surface which is not porous, whether the trophy is a silhouette on a piece of wood, a skin mount, or a cast. Shellac is satisfactory for this purpose; it is easy to apply and dries fast. Dilute white shellac 50–50 with commercial alcohol, which can be obtained at any paint shop. Refrain from excessive brushing, or brush streaks will appear. One coat is usually enough for skin mounts or casts produced in plastic-like materials. However, wood silhouettes and casts in plaster or casting compound may require more. Plaster usually takes several coats. Brush on one coat, wait until it dries, and then brush on the next—until a sheen or gloss appears which indicates that the plaster no longer absorbs the shellac. When the last coat dries, the trophy is ready for painting.

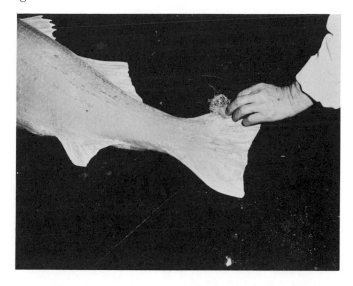

Fig. 102. The first step in painting a fish is to prepare the surface. Fill in any pinholes with plaster or a thick putty-like mixture of ordinary radiator silver paste. If plaster is used, go over the fish with sisal to smooth out any irregularities.

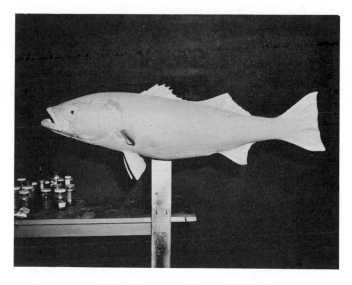

Fig. 103. Place the mount on a stand of convenient height for painting.

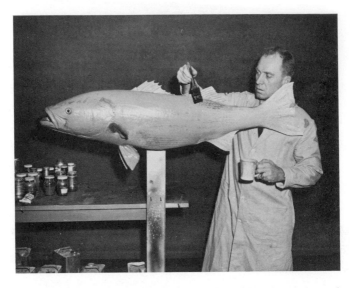

Fig. 104. Go over the entire fish with shellac diluted 50–50 with commercial alcohol.

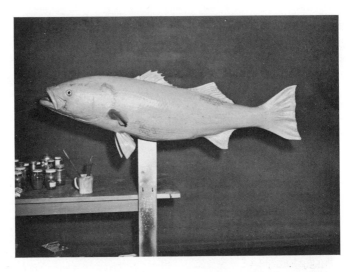

Fig. 105. Wait until the shellac is well dried before painting.

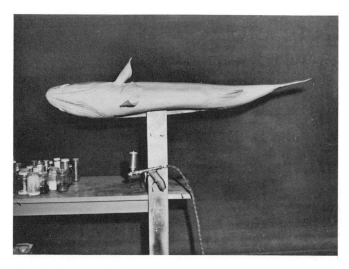

Fig. 106. Paint the belly side of the fish—nearly always a flat white.

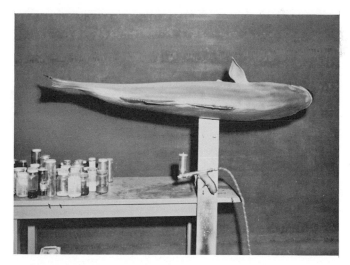

Fig. 107. Then turn the mount around and paint the dorsal surface—
usually bluish-green, brownish-green, or dark blue.

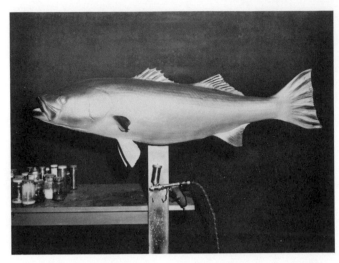

Fig. 108. Cover the lateral surface with pearl essence or chrome. Often
a light coat of flat white is applied first, as a base.

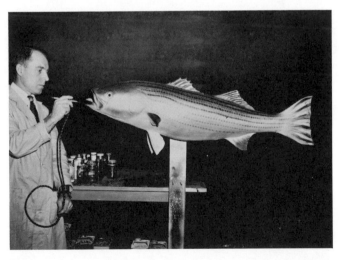

Fig. 109. Now put in the fine markings with a brush; or if using spray
lacquers, employ a small spray gun as the author is doing above.

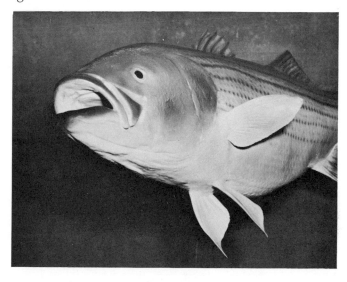

Fig. 110. Finally, put the finishing touches on the fins. If spraying the paint, place a paper in back of the fin to protect the body from paint.

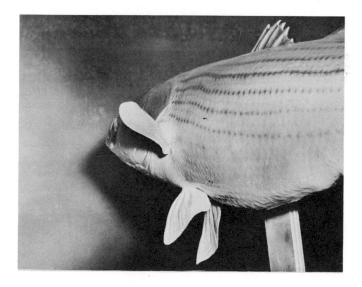

Fig. 111. In order to bring out the modeling (spines and rays), spray a bit of black or dark brown across the fin—almost in a parallel position so that the paint hits only the high spots.

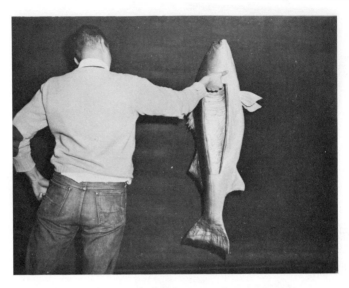

Fig. 112. The wall side of the fish need not be painted carefully since it won't be seen.

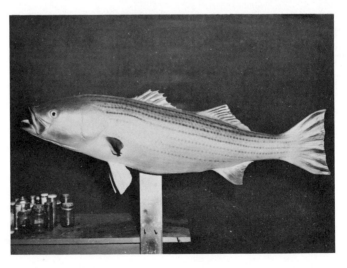

Fig. 113. The finished striped bass waiting to be varnished. It is a good idea to give it two coats. Be sure the first coat is thoroughly dry before applying the second.

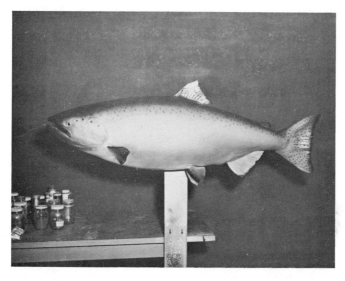

Fig. 114. A freshly painted king salmon. The fresh fish weighed 52 pounds and was taken by the author in Alaska.

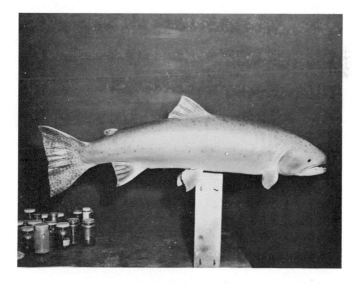

Fig. 115. A finished steelhead which was taken by a friend of the author, Larry Sheerin, at the Deschuttes River in Oregon where it comes into the Columbia. The fish weighed 21 pounds.

Simple Painting

In medallion-type trophies cast in plaster of Paris, wax, casting compound, or plastics, interesting and attractive results can be obtained by simple methods. For example, spray the entire mount with a copper, silver, or gold spray. These days this is a simple procedure. All paint stores carry handy little cans of all sorts of sprays which produce metallic effects. These sprays are inexpensive; many fish can be done with one can. They are easy to work by simply pressing a button or lever, and their substances dry quickly. The angler may like to experiment with bronze and oil colors to produce a patina effect (the green rust or aerugo that covers ancient bronze sculpture).

If the angler prefers something closer to the true color of his fish but does not have the talent to paint skillfully, he may delve into a stylized type of painting. For example, a yellow perch has a yellow body, black vertical bars, dark fins on top, and orange-pink ones on the belly side. Oil colors as they come out of the tube (plus a vehicle such as turpentine) can be used without any attempt at mixing pigment and attaining the gradations in coloration of a fine painting. However, the correct number of bars should be reproduced; and if a fish has spots, about the same number should be copied. In other words, a stylized method is a diagrammatic sort of painting which anyone can achieve. And results are surprising; about a half dozen species of fish done in this manner make an interesting and attractive collection.

Painting with Oils and Brush

If an attempt is made to reproduce the colors of the fish as closely as possible with oil colors and brush, notes or color transparencies, or both, should be taken of the fish as soon as possible after it comes out of the water.

Most fishes have a silvery base under the body colors which can be imitated by spraying chrome or silver over the mount before attempting to paint. Pearl essence is excellent for this purpose. Commercially, it is made mostly from scales of silvery fishes. Pearl essence is now available in synthetic form. This pastelike material must be mixed with lacquer and lacquer thinner. Of course, pigments should not be applied to the mount the same as to a canvas, for the oils are much too heavy and the mount would appear artificial. An oil color as it comes out of the tube cannot be used alone; it requires a vehicle to carry it smoothly over the area. A combination of linseed oil and turpentine makes an excellent vehicle. A type of linseed oil named "Stand Oil" is best; it has gone through a heating process which produces a thicker, more viscous oil. It has other desirable properties—pale color, less tendency toward after-yellowing, and a hard, durable finish. It also allows brush marks to flatten and disappear. The Stand Oil should be diluted with an equal amount of rectified (extra refined) pure, clear gum turpentine. Mix the color on a palette or other suitable surface, dip the brush into the vehicle (oil plus turpentine), then onto the oil color, and apply to the mount.

Every finished mount requires a hard, durable surface, such as varnish, as a protective coating. Allow the oil paints to dry thoroughly for a week or so before applying the varnish. Convenient spray cans of enamel or lacquer can be used. Clear varnish, brushed on, is also an excellent covering. Do not apply the first coat of any of these substances too heavily, or some of them may cause the paint on the mount to run. Artists' retouching varnish can be used safely over oils. It is a quick drying, light bodied, colorless varnish composed of selected pale resins. These materials can be obtained from any art shop.

Painting with Lacquer and Airbrush

Most professionals use lacquers and spray guns (compressed air) for painting fish mounts. An experienced worker can produce excellent results in a short time with this method. The lacquer dries almost instantly upon hitting the mount which, of course, is a great advantage; no dust adheres, and one color can be placed over another immediately to obtain depth and accuracy in color. Anyone having access to compressed air (some machines and tanks are small and portable) should try it.

Proceed in this manner: first, mix the paints. Small, instant coffee jars with screw tops serve admirably as receptacles. Pour 2 inches of lacquer thinner into the jar and squeeze in 2 or 3 inches of tube oil color into it. Mix well with a brush until the oil color has dissolved and is held in suspension. Add an equal amount (same as lacquer thinner) of clear lacquer; stir it. The mixture is now ready for the spray gun. Some brands of lacquer may be heavier than others. If the mixture is too heavy to go through the air gun smoothly, add more thinner. In other words, mix the color, thinner, and lacquer in proportion to suit the situation, although 50–50 lacquer and thinner usually works well.

First, spray the basic color—flat white, silver, or chrome—over the entire surface. Then, turn the mount on the support so that the belly can be sprayed easily (Fig. 106). The great majority of fishes have a flat white belly; therefore, a rather good load of white oil color should be included in the lacquer-thinner mix. On occasion, I may apply the white pigment from the tube with a brush dipped in lacquer directly to the belly of the fish—if results with the air gun are not "white" enough.

Now turn the fish around to a position which will bring the back or dorsal surface toward you (Fig. 107). Be careful not to touch the sprayed surface too soon. If the paint was applied a bit too heavily, it may still be wet. If your fingers have touched the mount in this condition, the paint will adhere to them. If this happens, it will be necessary to remove all paint and start over again!

Most fishes have a blue-green back. Therefore, spray the green on lightly and then go over it with blue; usually emerald green and Prussian blue are the best to use. A light spray of raw umber or raw sienna may be required, and then another touch of green over it. Now, attend to the side of the body with light sprays of the required colors. Do not apply the lacquer colors heavily or the basic silvery sheen will be lost. Up to this point, a medium-sized air gun may be used. For the finer painting required in doing the fins, jaws, cheek and body markings such as spots, bars, or lines, a small airbrush is required. When the paint job is completed, apply a couple of coats of clear varnish. Do not use lacquer for the finish coat because there is danger of the colors running. Lacquer with as little thinner as possible may be used, but still the colors underneath may run or soften because the heavier lacquer has time to affect them.

Painting the Glass Eye

Painted glass eyes can be purchased from most commercial taxidermy supply houses. Unpainted eyes are less expensive, however, and can be painted to match your fish with more accuracy. The blanks or unpainted eyes come with a dark pupil; therefore, only the iris requires painting.

Pour a bit of lacquer (not thinned) into the tin cap of a jar or other receptacle. Dip a small (⅛ inch) brush, which has stiff bristles, into the lacquer, then into a silver or gold powder, and dab the underside of the glass eye. Hold the eye along the edge, bottom side down, and dab the silver or gold (or both) from beneath so that you can see the results. Add more silver or gold as necessary. If the iris contained dark specks in life, include these with another small, stiff brush dipped in lacquer and touched to a dark oil pigment such as Vandyke brown. When satisfied that the paint job looks convincing, pour a few drops of lacquer (not thinned) over the back of the eye. Do not brush the lacquer on as the speckled effect of the iris might be softened. If fresh plastic is used to set the glass eye in the mount, drop hot wax over the lacquer for additional protection. Do this by holding a piece of beeswax over the eye and then touching the wax with a small hot tool. The wax will melt and drop over the eye.

6

Outlines and Silhouettes

The fun of angling includes the discussion and display of catches. Anglers love to establish permanent records of their prowess with rod and reel. For the angler who cannot spare the time or who perhaps does not possess the manual dexterity to produce a more complete type of trophy, I strongly suggest that he try one of the methods treated in this chapter.

All of these processes, even the most simple types, produce interesting results. I know. I have about sixty mounted fish in my home, some of which are exceptional fishes; yet my guests are most interested in a few art-board silhouettes of local fishes which adorn the walls of my tackle room. I suppose this is so because it stimulates a desire, present in the breast of every angler, to display his catches to his friends—and here is an easy, attractive way of doing it!

Pen and Ink Outlines

An outline record of a trophy fish may be a simple tracing in pencil on a piece of brown wrapping paper, which the angler may unroll or unfold to show his friends. With a bit more effort, however, a permanent, decorative piece can be produced instead.

First, wipe the excess slime off the fish. Place the specimen on a fairly heavy grade of brown paper or any other strong

paper and carefully trace the outline of the fish onto it using
a pencil with soft lead (Fig. 117). When making a tracing
around a fish, it is difficult to obtain a clean, smooth, detailed
outline; and no matter how well the fish is wiped some slime
will always remain on the paper. Therefore, the outline has to
be transferred to another piece of paper in order to remedy the
flaws. For this step I suggest a better grade of white paper
which will lie flat. The original outline can be cut out and used

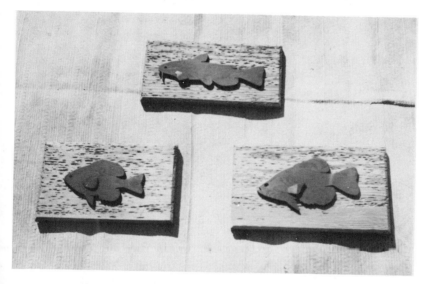

Fig. 116. Silhouettes cut out of wood and glued to a rustic backboard are
always attractive.

as a stencil for tracing the fish onto the white paper; carbon
paper can be used. If no carbon is handy, one can accomplish
similar results by covering the approximate area of the outline
on the back side of the brown paper with a pencil with a soft
grade of lead. Place the brown-paper outline over the white
paper and trace the drawing. Apply a bit of pressure with the
pencil, and the outline will be reproduced on the white paper.
The drawing on the white paper is still rough, so proceed to
smooth out irregular lines, erase here, add there, and in general
finish the outline. Perhaps you can improve the outline of your

trophy by using, as reference, a photo of your fish or an illustration in a good fishing book.

Now, with a pair of sharp scissors carefully cut out the outline of the fish. Center it on the final art board (art shops have a variety of stiff paper board you can choose from), and tack it lightly with masking tape in two or three places so that the cutout of the fish will not move. Trace it *lightly*. Remove the outline and touch up the sketch where necessary *lightly*. When you are satisfied that the drawing is final, go over it with pen and ink. The ink to use for this purpose is black drawing ink known as "India ink." The width of the line is a matter of preference. Line drawings in outline form look better when they are done in heavier lines. All art shops have a wide variety of pens for this purpose. It is not necessary to use the same line width throughout the entire drawing. You may like to put in finer lines for the fin spines and rays, the gill opening, etc.

Letter in the name of the angler, date, and place where the fish was caught. Enter this information either in the center of the fish or in one corner of the paper board. Your trophy outline will look handsome if you place a mat board frame, 2 or 3 inches wide, around it. A first-class job can be achieved by finishing the project with a wooden frame containing a glass.

If the angler prefers, the fish can be a solid silhouette rather than an outline. This is accomplished by simply filling in the drawing with India ink. Use a soft brush for this purpose.

Art Board Silhouettes

Any angler with a bit of artistic sense can enjoy producing trophy silhouettes of fish in art board. Art shops carry a variety of interesting paper boards such as mat, illustration, bristol, and poster boards. Many different shades of color, including gold and silver, and different finishes are available.

Reproduce the outline of the fish as described in detail above. When the outline is finished on the art board, cut it out with a single-edge razor blade or any other suitable sharp instrument. In order to protect the table or desk top on which you

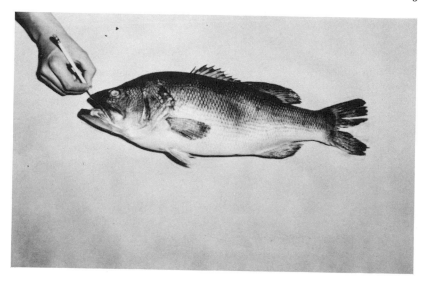

Fig. 117. Place the specimen on a fairly heavy grade of brown paper, or any other strong paper, and carefully trace the outline onto it using a pencil with soft lead.

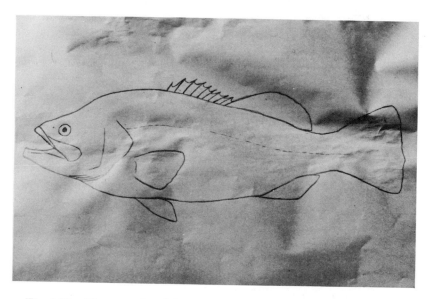

Fig. 118. The completed first draft outline of the largemouth bass.

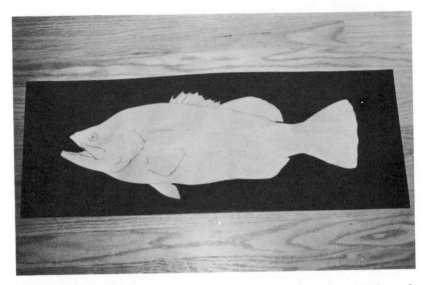

Fig. 119. The paper fish has been cut out and placed on black cardboard. Next, a tracing is made onto the cardboard.

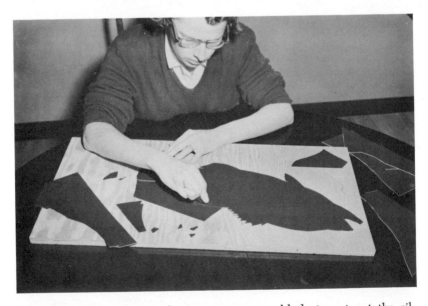

Fig. 120. The author's wife, Bo, uses a razor blade to cut out the silhouette. If the edge of the black cardboard is gray or white, brush black India ink over it.

are working, place a piece of glass, wood, or cardboard under-neath the art board before using the razor blade.

Before you browse through the materials in the art shop, have an idea of what you are looking for. First, select the wall on which the silhouette mount is to be displayed. Is it pine paneled? If so, is the paneling stained, or is it a natural finish? Is the wall blue—light blue or dark blue?

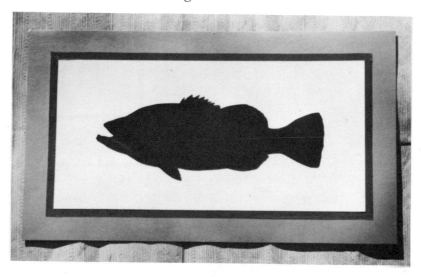

Fig. 121. Another trophy largemouth bass—black on white with a gold frame.

Color Combinations

It is an interesting job to select the colors of your trophy silhouette so that they will not clash with the color of the walls and the room décor. If the colors are not right, your silhouette mount will look terrible. But if they are correct your trophy will not only look great, but it will also be an important con-tribution to the color scheme of the room. If you are a boy, get your mother and dad in on the project. If you are a hus-band, consult your wife for her ideas on color combinations. You will be amazed how much easier it is to get your trophy on the wall if you ask her advice on colors!

Some colors go together nicely; others do not. Anglers who have had no experience in art may find the color circle or wheel (Fig. 122) useful for choosing color combinations for fish silhouettes. The color circle is generally accepted as the basic guide in presenting one color with another.

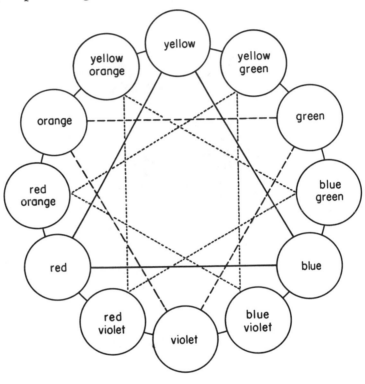

PRIMARY TRIAD———

SECONDARY TRIAD— — — —

HUES TRIAD⋯⋯⋯⋯⋯⋯

Fig. 122. Color wheel. See Color Combinations in Chapter 6.

I believe it will not be amiss to discuss color a bit more. Invariably when considering color, the word "spectrum" pops up. The spectrum is a continuously varying band of color—red, orange, yellow, green, blue, indigo, and violet. In other words, the spectrum contains, in blended sequence, all colors visible to the eye. In nature the spectrum is a rainbow.

All the colors in the spectrum are made from three colors: *red, yellow,* and *blue.* Therefore, these are known as the *primary* colors. Any two of the primaries combined produce a *secondary* color: red + yellow = *orange;* blue + yellow = *green;* red + blue = *violet.*

The mixing of adjoining colors on the color circle can be carried to more than five hundred varieties.

Basically, there are four types of color combinations or color schemes—complementary, analogous, triad, and monochromatic. These combinations or schemes consist of colors that go well together when used in decorating, and they are equally applicable to art-board fish silhouette trophies.

1. Complementary Color Scheme
   This setup is called complementary because one color is complemented by a combination of two colors which are equidistant from it on the color wheel. For example, take red; mix the two colors equidistant from it on the wheel (yellow and blue) and you will find its complement to be green. More pleasing effects are usually obtained, however, if the two colors are not of the same intensity. If, for instance, you choose a brilliant red, rather than choosing a brilliant green to accompany it, select a lighter green—that is, a green mixed with white.

2. Analogous Color Scheme
   Any three colors adjacent to each other on the wheel are analogous, for example, the two colors analogous to yellow would be yellow-green and green (they both contain yellow). Two other colors analogous to yellow are orange and yellow-orange, (both also contain yellow). Here, too, all three colors should not be used in the same intensity—rather, one brilliant and two light or one light and the other grayed.

3. Triad Color Scheme
   Three colors equidistant on the wheel, such as orange, green, and violet form a triad (again no three of the same intensity). This scheme offers variation without clashing of colors.

4. Monochromatic Color Scheme

One color with two or more values of the same color produces a monochromatic color scheme. For example, a light green silhouette on a dark green background.

As I said previously, the color scheme of your room should be the basic criterion for choice of color in your fish silhouette. If you have green walls, your fish may look well cut from an illustration board on the red or maroon side (complementary colors). The background board could be a green lighter or darker than the wall.

If you want a more subtle effect in your room with the green walls, your fish could be a blue-green silhouette or a yellow-green background board (analogous colors).

On a blue wall you might choose a maroon fish on a pale yellow background (colors in triad). If you were looking for a still softer effect on the blue wall, you could choose a light blue silhouette (lighter than the walls) and a very light blue background (monochromatic colors).

Use the colors in the wheel and my suggestions merely as a guide. The final choice should be made mainly by considering the color of the walls, rugs, and all other accessories in the room. Wise choice of a wooden frame may also improve the composition of your silhouette mount. Try different combinations by placing pieces of colored paper against the wall. You will find it fun.

The main wall in my basement tackle room is made of cinderblocks which I have painted light green. Another wall is paneled with stained driftwood. On the green wall I have a series of three fish trophy silhouettes—brown, rainbow, and brook trout. The fish are cut from light maroon illustration board on a white background of poster board, and each is encompassed in a 3-inch frame of dark green mat board. The driftwood wall has a single silhouette—a largemouth bass which is done in gold on a black background with a white frame of mat board. All of them are set in dark wooden frames which have a natural rubbed finish. Each fish has the weight, dimensions, place where caught, and date lettered in black India ink in the right-hand corner. Without fail, every one of my fishing friends and every new member of the Yale Fishing Club that sees my fish-mount silhouettes for the first time exclaims, "This is wonderful; I'm going to start a collection too!"

Outlines Burnt in Wood

Fish trophies produced in wood go well in a casual or rustic type of room. A series of fish outlines burnt in wooden plaques add interest to any informal room whether it is the den at home, a boy's room, or the main room of a fishing camp. The fishes outlined may be of several different species, or the display may consist of a single kind.

You and your family may fish in an area that has several species of fish (for example: bluegill, sunfish, catfish, yellow perch, bass, and pickerel; or along the shore: tautog, cunner, flatfish, bluefish, striped bass, etc.). Have a family competition. Father can be weigh-master and recorder; of course the rest of the family should witness the weighing-in of any fish he catches! A temporary outline of each fish entered is made. As a heavier fish comes in, another outline is traced; and the previous record discarded. At the end of each season, the biggest fish of each species is permanently recorded with its outline burnt in a plaque. The angler's name, date, and place where the fish was caught should also be burnt in. It could be great fun to have the final party of the season reserved for the wall hanging of the outline trophies.

George Albrecht and I stayed at a fishing camp, on the banks of the Miramichi River in New Brunswick, Canada, where we took great interest in the burnt-in outlines of Atlantic salmon that lined the walls. Every salmon over 15 pounds taken by anglers who stayed at this camp was burnt directly into the wood of the wall. Each outline was accompanied by the name of the angler and the fly which took the fish. This collection was unusual because the silhouettes dated back many years.

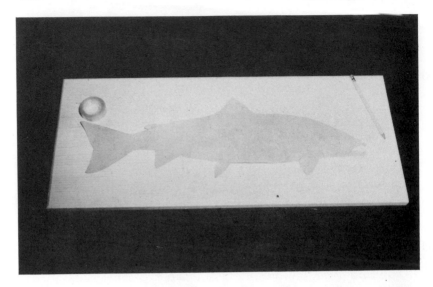

Fig. 123. For a burnt-in outline make the paper cutout as previously described. Tape the cutout of the fish to a piece of white wood or white pine, and trace around it.

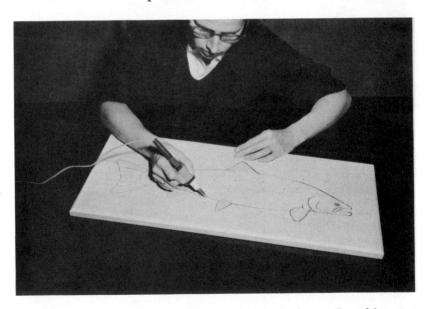

Fig. 124. Burn the outline into the wood with an electric "wood burning pen."

If you intend to make a burnt outline trophy on a plaque, choose a good grade of wood without knots. Clear white pine is fine for this purpose. Outline the fish as described earlier. Be sure to make the initial outlines on paper and then transfer them onto the wood. Otherwise, the wood will absorb some of the slime of the fish and thus be discolored.

My friend Larry Sheerin of San Antonio, Texas and I visited Enrique Guerra at his ranch in Mexico. Larry and I watched

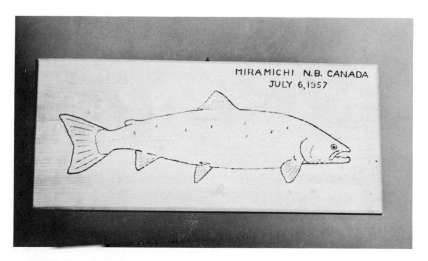

Fig. 125. The finished outline trophy of a grilse (salmon).

fascinated as Enrique burnt designs into the walls of his dining room. He had a low fire going in the fireplace, where he heated large branding irons until red hot and then pressed them, sizzling, into the wall. However, I would not advise anyone to try this method on fish silhouettes. An electrical tool is made specifically for this type of work; it is easy to handle, heats quickly, and is inexpensive. The price is usually about three dollars for a set which includes the main heating unit with a cord attached to it and about six interchangeable pens of different shapes. Commercially, an outfit of this type is known as a "wood burning pen," or an "electrical pencil set." **All art**

supply stores and hobby shops carry them. If you own a small
soldering iron it may be used instead; but it is a bit awkward
to employ because the handle of the soldering iron is high,
thus making it hard to manage.

The thickness of the line is a matter of taste. Practice a bit
on a piece of scrap wood with the different points before
attempting the fish outline. It is better to go over the entire
fish lightly several times, rather than to attempt to burn the
line deeply into the wood at the first burning. Of course, always
apply the stain or varnish to the plaque when all the burning
is finished. A fish trophy of this type does not look well with
a glossy finish, and the wood looks best natural. Brush on a
thin coat of shellac (thinned 50–50 with alcohol). When that
is dry apply a coat or two of rubbed-effect varnish (satin finish),
available at any paint store.

Wood Silhouettes

Another easy but satisfying way of making a fish trophy collection is to cut the silhouettes out of wood. Here, again, is a
method that can satisfy a wide range of individual abilities.

Fish silhouettes in wood can be an excellent project for
boys who like to fish and who also like to handle tools. The
outline should be produced on the wood as described previously. If the boy is just learning to handle tools, I would suggest ¼-inch plywood for the fish silhouette. The wood can be
clamped to a table to make sawing easier, or it can be held by
hand as shown in Fig. 128. The edges of the fish should be
sanded, and the spot for the eye can be drilled. Stain the silhouette and glue it to a ½-inch pine plaque with beveled edges.

Any angler who is handy with tools can have fun making a
series of wooden silhouette trophies which require more care.
For example, the silhouette can be produced from ¾- to 1-inch
stock. A power jig saw or band saw should be used. The
edges of the wooden fish can be beveled with a rasp, or the
edges can be rasped until a "half round" effect is achieved. The
eye should be hollowed out with a drill. The lines denoting

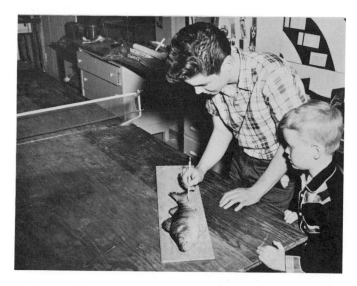

Fig. 126. Ronnie Johnson outlines a big yellow perch which was caught
by his younger brother, Keith.

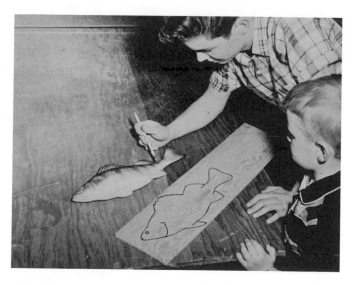

Fig. 127. The outline as it appears on a piece of ¼-inch plywood.

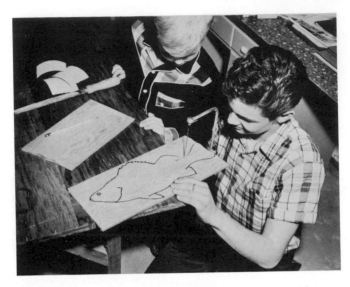

Fig. 128. Ronnie shows Keith how to cut out the fish.

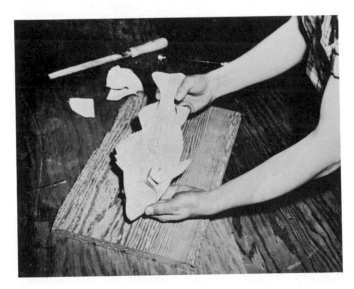

Fig. 129. The edges of the wooden perch are filed and sanded. A pectoral fin is glued on.

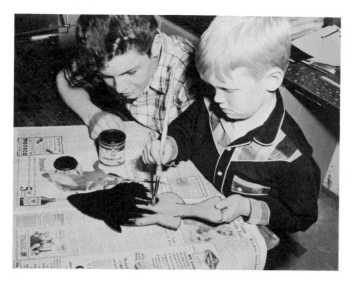

Fig. 130. Keith paints the fish.

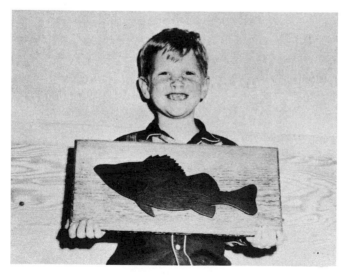

Fig. 131. Because he has caught the biggest yellow perch in the Johnson family of anglers, Keith is proclaimed champion.

the gill opening, jaws, fin rays, and so forth can be carved in with appropriate tools. Another way is to cut out just the body and tail of the fish, and then insert the fins which have been sawed from material such as ¼-inch plywood. In this case, slits in the wooden body will have to be gouged out—use a drill and then a chisel. Also, leave a base on the fins which can be inserted into the recesses and held with glue. A glass eye glued in will also give the trophy added sparkle. This type of trophy looks good stained dark if placed on a light colored wall, and a natural finish is best if it is situated on a dark wall. I prefer such a silhouette without a backboard or plaque. Letter the pertinent information directly onto the body of the wooden fish, black lettering on a natural wood fish or white lettering on a fish stained dark. A thin coat of shellac (thinned 50–50 with alcohol) should be applied over the stain before painting on the lettering. Complete the trophy with a coat of flat-finish varnish.

7

Photographs as Trophies

Any angler who carries a camera during fishing trips can build a fine collection of fish pictures. Notice, I did not say fishing pictures. I have viewed thousands of photographs taken by all types of anglers whose results ranged from the ridiculous to photos which indicated professional ability. Almost without exception the photos are either beautiful scenes of the outdoors with the angler as the secondary point of interest, or else the proud angler is standing stiffly, holding the fish in one hand and the rod awkwardly in the other. Most anglers, when posing for a photo, stand against brick buildings, clapboard, fences, and other uncomplimentary backgrounds with dominating horizontal lines. However, with a bit of coaching—and some common sense—any angler can produce excellent photo trophies.

Composition and Hints

All fishermen love to be photographed with their catch. I'm included. I am not ashamed to say that I have a great many photos of myself with fish of all kinds. However, I attempt to set up the composition so that the photo will have as little appearance as possible of being posed. For example, if you catch a big trout, don't pose stiffly. Try something like this: sit on a rock at the edge of the stream, put the open creel beside you, and hold the fish in your hands as though you are

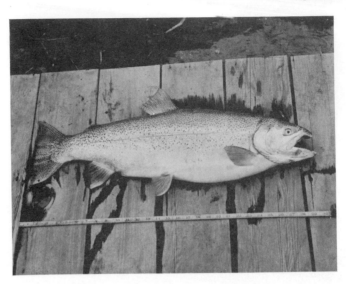

Fig. 132. A 12-pound Alaskan rainbow (all fishes in this series of photos were caught by the author). This photo could have been improved by lowering the fish on the platform to eliminate the ground above it. The tape has been added to prove that the fish is 30 inches long.

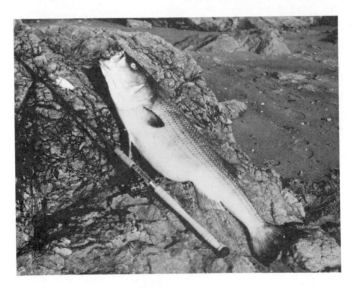

Fig. 133. This photo of a 42-pound striped bass is given character by posing the fish on a rock.

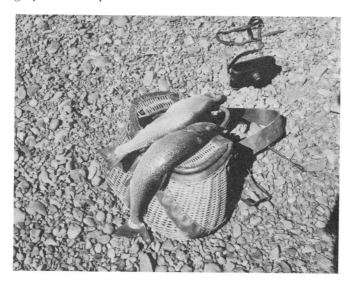

Fig. 134. Montana cutthroats are placed over a creel on the shores of a pebbly stream. An object such as a camera can be positioned strategically to improve the photo composition.

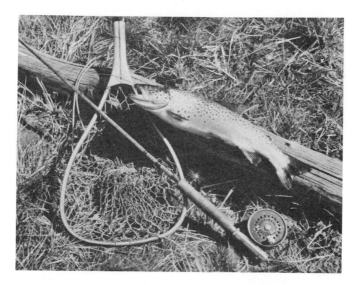

Fig. 135. A brown trout taken in Encampment, Wyoming was posed on the rail of a broken cattle fence. Notice how the wide landing net balances the long narrow lines of the fence rail and rod.

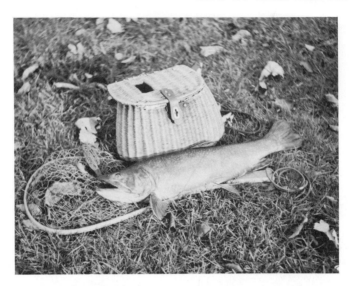

Fig. 136. Here again the creel supplies the bulk necessary to balance the long lines of the Canadian brook trout's body and the landing net.

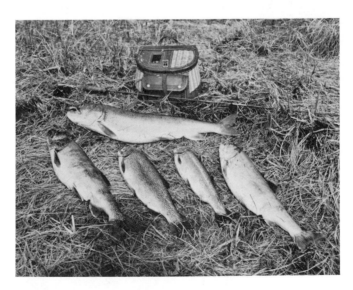

Fig. 137. Although a single fish is best for a trophy photo, occasionally a pleasing group composition may be produced, as with the above Alaskan fishes—mackinaw (lake trout), rainbow, and dolly varden.

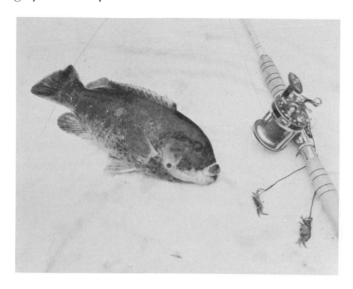

Fig. 138. This Rhode Island tautog makes a fine photo on a piece of canvas. It is always interesting to show the bait or the lure that took the fish.

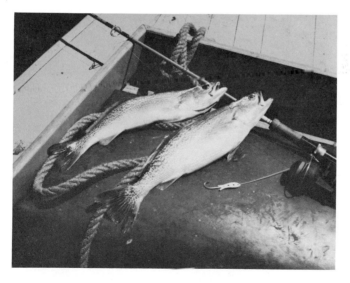

Fig. 139. A brace of weakfish taken in Connecticut. Notice the interesting lines of the boat. I placed the rope there to give the photo added character.

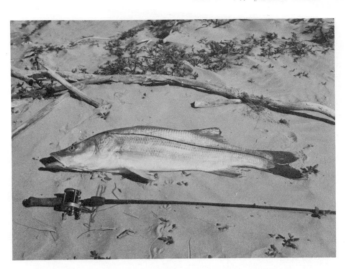

Fig. 140. Although this photo of a snook on a Mexican beach is sharp and in fine exposure, it is not a good picture because all three lines—driftwood, fish, and rod—are parallel. The photo could have been greatly improved by simply turning the rod or stick, or both, to other angles. Another improvement—the rod could have been turned around so that the handle and reel were on the right side, by the tail.

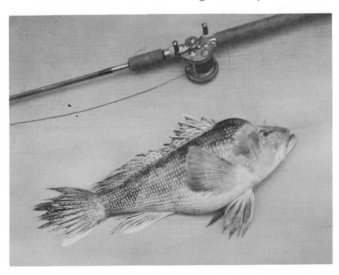

Fig. 141. Fish always look bigger when the comparing object, the rod and reel, is behind it. A male (hump) seabass.

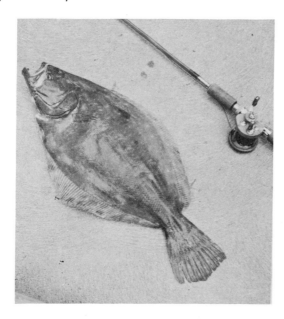

Fig. 142. A fluke taken off Hampton Bays, Long Island. The wide oval shaped, flat body of the fish goes well with the long narrow form of the rod.

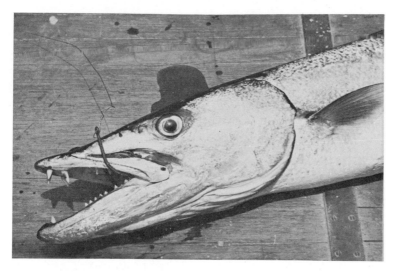

Fig. 143. Close-ups are always successful. A Florida barracuda.

admiring it. Make it appear as if this is a few minutes' break in the fishing. And don't look at the camera! Think of the composition. Is there another boulder which will balance the other side of the photo? Move over a few feet; perhaps a branch of a tree overhead will add interest., A few extra minutes required for a good shot will pay great dividends in pleasing results. If you want the fish to be the point of interest— and it should be in a trophy photo—have the camera close to the angler and the fish. A profile shot of the angler, including his head and chest, as he looks down on the prize is an excellent way to portray both.

However, for a good series of fish trophy photos, one which will dignify any room from the casual or rustic to more formal settings, I strongly recommend elimination of the angler from the photo. Black and white photographs lend themselves better to a line or grouped series of fish photos. Colored prints are best for a single picture in one given area of wall space.

Do not place your fish just anywhere on the ground for a shot. If you want to indicate the size of the fish, place your catch so that there is a natural object to compare the fish with. Don't place a package of cigarettes or a tape measure alongside the fish. Instead, arrange the fish on a log or over a creel. Lay the rod beside it, or perhaps place your hat, a fly box, or a plug alongside. An interesting shot consists of laying the fish across a landing net; another example—set the fish in a spot along the shore so that a portion of its body lies in the water. Sometimes the fish looks best without accessories, propped on an interesting piece of pebbly shore or sandy beach. Do not take the shot from an unnecessary distance from the fish; fill a good portion of the camera finder with the subject. There are countless arrangements which will prove interesting and artistic. Take a few minutes to look around; give it some thought.

Volumes have been written on cameras, their manipulation, and the actual techniques of photography, so I won't advise the angler on that score. All photography shops stock manuals on photography. Because I have been photographing fish in the field for many years, however, I might add that there are a few simple things that the angler-photographer should keep in mind in order to produce the best kind of trophy photos:

1. Get close to the fish.
2. Look for an interesting composition or arrangement of the subject.
3. Move your camera angle until you find a spot where the least reflection is bouncing back from the body of the glossy fish.
4. Try three or four different exposures of the same shot.

I have found that a series of black and white photos look best if they are all mounted identically—usually with a rather wide mat board and a narrow black wooden frame. My brother, Fritz, has a series of six fresh-water fish done in this manner in his study. The photos are placed in a single line about 16 inches above the wainscoting. I must say they look great. Figures 132 to 143 may suggest composition possibilities to anglers.

8

Special Trophies

Properly preserved and displayed, various original parts of fishes make fascinating trophies. There is something about a head of a fish preserved dry or in Formalin that draws immediate attention. A collection of tails, whether dried or cast, make an unusual display. Head mounts, of course, always have been popular. And bills or spears of big game fishes have been collected by fishermen since time immemorial. One of my hobbies is collecting the bills of sailfish and making letter-openers of them.

Fish Heads Preserved

A series of heads, preserved dry, make an interesting collection. The heads can be mounted on plaques for wall decoration, or they can be displayed on shelves. Heads of fishes such as pike, pickerel, barracuda, and bluefish are especially interesting because of their imposing teeth.

Cut the head from the body close behind the edge of the gill cover, taking care not to disengage the tongue. I prefer to remove the gills, although they may be left in the head. Clean out the inside of the skull and cut away loose flesh and bone. It is not necessary to cut away all of the skull as in a skin mount. It is a good idea, however, to break a hole through

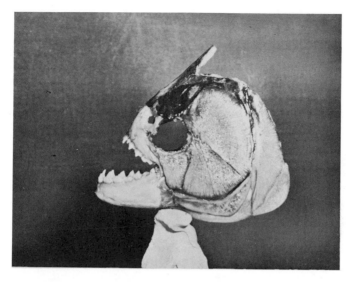

Fig. 144. Only the bony structure of this piranha head remains. Notice how the skin has been cut away to display the teeth fully.

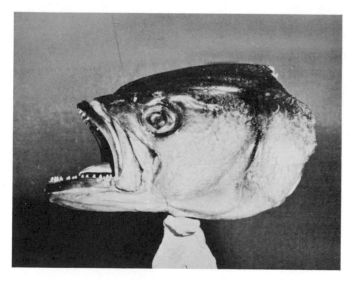

Fig. 145. A dried head of a bluefish after it had been preserved in a 10 per cent solution of Formalin.

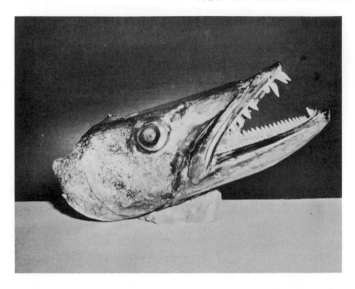

Fig. 146.   Fish such as pike, pickerel, or barracuda (above) make interesting trophy heads because of their imposing teeth.

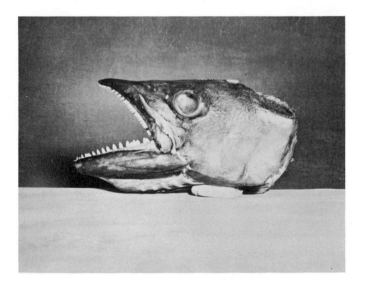

Fig. 147.   A king mackerel (kingfish) head also draws attention.

here and there to remove the brain and to facilitate the entrance of the preservative solution.

Prop the mouth open with a piece of wood or wire, and place the head in a 10 per cent solution of Formalin (nine parts water to one part Formalin). It should remain immersed a week or two to allow thorough impregnation by the Formalin. Remove the head and permit it to dry gradually in open air. Do not try to rush the drying by placing the head over a radiator or setting it in the sun. When the head has dried hard, a matter of a couple of weeks, cover it with two or three coats of enamel or lacquer. Small spray cans of these are obtainable at any paint shop. The eyes can be replaced with glass eyes. However, since a dried head is not meant to look alive, I usually let the eyes remain, to dry also. The head can be secured to a stained and varnished base for easier handling. Drill small holes through the lower jaws and attach the head to the base with wire.

Another interesting way of preserving heads is to remove as much of the flesh as possible, leaving only the bony structure. This can be done with a fresh head or with a Formalin specimen. If a fresh head is used, it is advisable to place the bony structure in Formalin for a few days anyway, after it is cleaned. The head can be left in its natural state or sprayed with gold or silver.

Fish Tails Preserved

Tails of all types of fishes are easily preserved. Immersion in a 10 per cent solution of Formalin for a week or so is all that is necessary. Allow the tail to dry gradually in open air; do not place it in the sun or over a radiator. The tail can then be attached to a plaque, or it can be hung on the wall by a concealed wire. Another attractive method (for a big fish) is to tie a ¼-inch rope around the base of the tail, leaving a loop for attachment to a metal wall hanger.

Tails of large fish such as tuna, marlin, and sailfish are especially imposing trophies when dried and painted. The famous

Cabo Blanco Fishing Club in Peru, where the largest game fishes in the world are taken, has a most impressive driveway in front of the clubhouse—it is lined with posts that have large marlin tails attached to their tops (Fig. 148).

A plastic or resin cast of any fish tail, painted in the original colors, is especially effective. It can be attached to a plaque, and the angler's information can be painted on or inscribed in metal by an engraver.

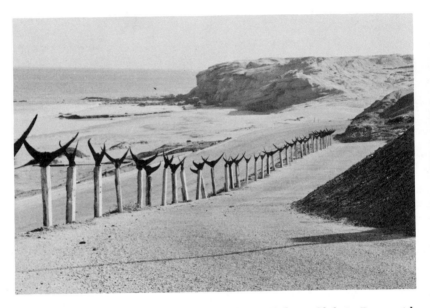

Fig. 148. The driveway of the Cabo Blanco Fishing Club in Peru, with a fence of posts on which marlin tails are mounted.
(Photo by Kip Farrington)

Head Mounts

Head mounts of fishes are often preferable to full-body mounts, especially of big game fishes such as swordfish, marlin, and sharks. The medium-sized fishes—large striped bass, bluefish, catfish, musky, pike, and bass—also make attractive head mounts.

The same procedure is followed in making a head mold as in producing a regular two-piece body mold, except, of course, that the plaster need not extend more than half the length of the body. Always include the pectoral fin or fins and a portion of the body beyond the fins. Wherever possible (depending on the type of fish), include a portion of the dorsal fin. It is al-

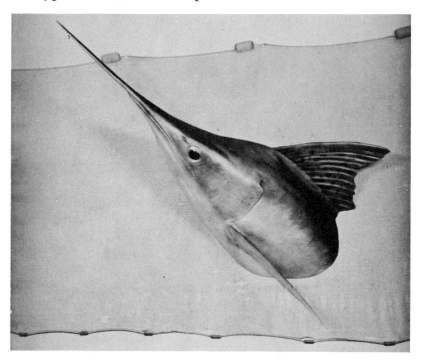

Fig. 149. One of my proudest possessions is the hollow cast of my first striped marlin taken many years ago in New Zealand. The mold was made on the New Zealand beach while the cast was produced at home.

ways preferable to make the mold longer than the intended cast, so that the cast or mount may be cut to fit at the desired angle against the wall. This is easier than attempting to make the mold exact. Often a regular body mold that has not been severely damaged when the cast was removed can be used again for producing a head mount. The cast can be made from synthetic materials or from casting compound.

A head mount which faces out from the wall at an angle is more attractive than a mount facing head-on. However, I have made some unusually interesting large catfish heads that were mounted facing directly away from the wall. After the cast has been cut at the desired angle, attach a wooden backboard along its back edges with flat-headed screws countersunk below the surface of the cast. Hide the screw heads with some of the material of which the cast is made.

Bills or Spears of Big Fishes

The preserved bills or spears of big fishes—sailfish, marlin, swordfish, and sawfish—make excellent trophies. They are comparable to the mounted antlers loved by deer hunters. See Figs. 150, 151, and 153 for ways of displaying these trophies.

Swordfish. When an angler catches a swordfish, he never releases it, because the flesh of this fish is always in demand and usually brings high prices. Therefore, the angler nearly always cuts the sword off and retains its as a trophy.

Preservation of the sword is simple; actually it requires only drying. As the sword is mostly bony in structure, it may simply be sawed off from the head and then exposed to the air to dry. In drying, the sword will lose some of its original color. Some anglers paint the sword as close to the natural color as possible and then apply several coats of lacquer.

If a couple of holes are drilled along one edge and a chain attached, the sword can be hung on a wall (Fig. 150). If the angler prefers to have the trophy in an upright position on a shelf or table, a piece of wood should be attached to the base of the sword (Fig. 151).

Some anglers prefer to clean or bleach the sword so that it appears whitish. This can be done by simply immersing the sword in salt water, but this procedure requires much time in soaking. A better method of bleaching is to place the sword in a 1 or 2 per cent solution of potassium hydroxide for about a week in sunshine. The fleshy material will be broken down,

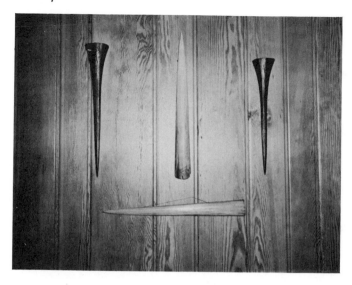

Fig. 150. Swordfish and marlin bills can be situated to advantage on walls.

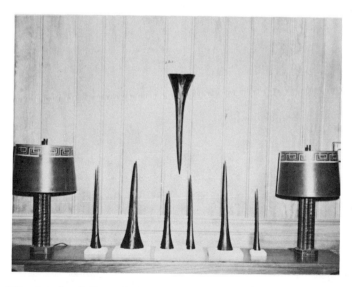

Fig. 151. Marlin bills make attractive trophies, either on the wall or mounted upright on blocks of wood. *Top:* Black marlin. *Left to right:* Pacific sailfish, black marlin, an unusually stubby bill of a blue marlin, white marlin, striped marlin, and Atlantic sailfish.

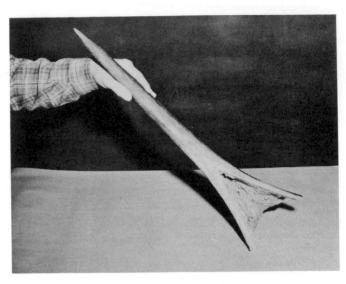

Fig. 152. The underside of a black marlin bill. The upper fleshy fore part of the mouth has been removed and only the bony or hard portion remains.

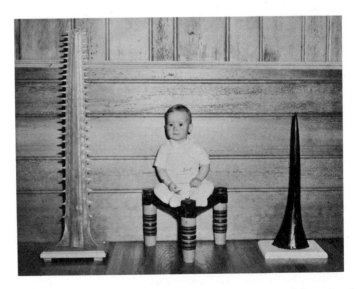

Fig. 153. My son, Tom, sits between the bills of a sawfish and a black marlin to emphasize their size.

leaving the bone whitish. When removed from the solution, the sword should be washed in fresh water and dried.

Sawfish. The sawfish should not be confused with the swordfish. The swordfish has a pointed, smooth-edged bill. The sawfish's bill has a snub end and about twenty-five sharp, toothlike protuberances along each side of the two lateral edges. Skates and rays are closely related to the sawfish.

A large sawfish is dangerous when being boated. Its toothed bill is a formidable weapon. For this reason, the sawfish's "saw" is a conversation-provoking trophy which all anglers love. It can be given the same preservative treatment as described for the swordfish bill.

My pal Larry Sheerin and I had a hair-raising experience with a big sawfish off the outlet of Laguna Madre in Mexico. We had watched the huge fish, which looked like a vast shadow, working the shallows when we were fishing for tarpon. We returned in the afternoon to the same area with some big-game tackle; and the sawfish, still lurking there, took the half of a spotted weakfish Larry had on for bait. It's a longer story than I can relate here—we got involved with some sharks while fighting the sawfish. As an illustration for this book, I photographed the bill of that sawfish, which I have mounted on a stand, alongside my son Tom, to demonstrate the impressive size of the bill or saw (Fig. 153).

Marlin and Sailfish. The marlin and the sailfish are the most spectacular big-game acrobats in the sea. Any angler fortunate enough to experience fighting one of these beauties certainly would like to have at home some sort of memento of the occasion. It is a comparatively rare angler who has the facilities to accommodate more than one or two mounts, if any, of these big fish on his walls. Therefore, the bills from marlin and sailfish make excellent trophies.

Marlin are nearly always boated because they are not too common. Everywhere that I have fished for marlin, they have been gladly accepted as food by the local people—except off our American coasts. Anglers who catch sailfish in the vicinity of Florida are asked to release their fish as a conservation measure, unless the fish is to be used as a trophy. However, smoked sailfish is gaining in popularity. Also, scientists have found that the sailfish has a short life span and its release may not be as important as previously thought. In the future more sailfish may be taken ashore.

The bill of a marlin or a sailfish looks much better if it includes a base rather than just the bill proper. Saw off the bill part way up the head, about an inch or so in front of the eye. Cut away the roof of the mouth—you may need a hack saw—and remove all the insides with a knife. A chisel is useful in gouging out the bony material and gristle. Work away until the bony structure of the bill proper is reached and just a shell of the base remains (Fig. 152).

After cleaning out the base, rub the inside with salt. Set the bill aside, well salted, in a pan overnight. This procedure will assist in drawing out the juices. Scrape away some more at the base and then wash off the salt. Usually, some grease will remain in the base; therefore, it is a good idea to soak the bill for a few days in a strong detergent or other liquid which has the power to remove the grease but will not harm the bill. Although not always necessary, it is a good idea to place the bill in a 10 per cent solution of Formalin (nine parts water to one part Formalin) for a few days. Allow the bill to dry thoroughly before mounting.

It is difficult to saw off the bill from the head in such a manner that the base is square—that is, so that when placed in an upright position on a table the bill will be perfectly perpendicular to the table top. For this reason, some additional cutting with a hack saw or a rasp will be necessary later.

The bill makes a better appearance if the base is filled. One method is to fill it with plaster of Paris. Make a heavy mixture of the plaster—like stiff whipped cream—so that it will stay where placed with a trowel. If the bill is to be hung on a wall, insert a looped wire into the plaster while it is still soft. Wait until the plaster is thoroughly dry before applying a couple of coats of shellac to it. Then paint the bill in its natural colors, dark blue on the dorsal surface and light gray or flesh color underneath.

A better way of finishing the base is to cut a piece of ⅛- or ¼-inch wire mesh the shape of the base, and place it in position so that it encloses the bottom and underside. The edges of the wire can be bent in such a way as to hold the mesh firmly in place. Now cut a piece of cheesecloth the same shape. Press casting compound (mixed liberally with plaster and water) into the cheesecloth with a putty knife, and then cover the wire mesh with the cheesecloth. When this has set, apply more compound and model the material here and there until it is smooth and finished. Wait until thoroughly dry before shellacking and painting. If the blil is intended to stand upright, trowel some fresh compound onto the bottom of the base and press it down firmly on a greased piece of glass. In this manner the base will be perfectly flat. The grease or Vaseline will prevent it from sticking to the glass. If the bill is to be hung on a wall, insert a looped wire into the base.

Shark Jaws

Sharks, like snakes, are unusually interesting to everyone, even though most people may abhor them. These animals have an unexplainable attraction, perhaps because they are considered to be dangerous and repulsive. Whatever the cause may be, the fact remains that a photo or even just a mention of the word "shark" draws immediate attention. Therefore, the jaws of a shark mounted on an attractive plaque make an excellent trophy. Place a set on your wall and you will soon discover that your guests will make a beeline toward the shark jaws, even though you may have more valuable objects in evidence.

No shark has a true bone in its body. The skeleton is composed of cartilaginous material. The jaws are not hard bone; therefore, care must be exercised when cutting them out of the head. If you cannot work on the jaws immediately, sever the head with a knife and a saw. Dispose of the body over the side,

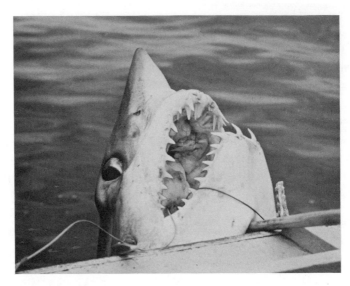

Fig. 154. A 321-pound mako shark taken by the author in New Zealand.

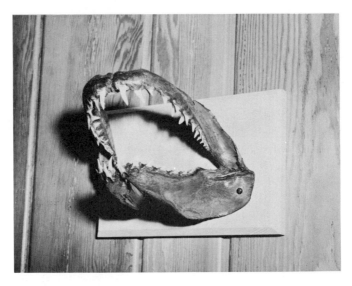

Fig. 155. The jaws of the same fish in the author's tackle room at home.

unless, in the case of a mako shark, you want to cut some steaks from the carcass.

Be sure the shark is dead before you attempt to decapitate him! This is not as silly as it sounds. The shark's jaws which appear in Fig. 155 belonged to a 321-pound mako I caught off the Bay of Islands in New Zealand. We boated that beast shortly after 10:00 A.M. and lashed him securely atop the stern. His back was lanced severely in a dozen places by our over-enthusiastic mate. The fish was fully exposed to the broiling sun the rest of the day, while we fished. We returned to Otehei Lodge about 7:00 P.M. and hoisted the mako onto the dock with a rope and pulley. Then I posed myself proudly, with a rod and reel, by the shark, which was hanging tail-up, close to the edge of the dock. Just as the photographer was about to take the last shot, the shark suddenly came to life; and with an amazing twist in his body, snapped his jaws—at me, I thought. His sudden action took me by such surprise that I dropped the rod and tried to jump back. There was a 6- by 6-inch railing at my feet so that when I attempted to move, my heels caught the railing. I went overboard! I didn't mind the water so much because I was ready for a bath anyway; but there were some pretty girls watching me as I posed with my chest stuck out, and it was embarrassing. Since that memorable event, I've had the greatest respect for sharks!

Let us assume that the angler has had no unpleasant experience and still wishes to remove the jaws. A sharp knife is essential. Do not attempt to cut through the hide to get at the jaws. Instead, start cutting from inside the mouth. Keep slicing through the flesh and skin from the teeth downward in the lower jaw. Do not use the knife too ambitiously or the cartilaginous jaw will be cut.

When separation is complete around the outer side of the lower jaw, turn the head around and repeat the process with the upper jaw. With some pulling and cutting of gristle and cartilage, here and there, the jaws will come away from the main body of the head. Do *not* disengage the jaws where they meet at the angle. Now commence to cut along the inside, starting from the angle of the jaw and working forward. Cut and scrape away all bits of meat and gristle that may be adhering to the jaws, and then rub salt on them and let it stay overnight. The salt will draw out the juices and the next day the extra matter adhering to the jaws can be scraped away more easily. Rinse the jaws in clean water and lay aside to dry. Prop the jaws apart with pieces of wood while drying, or the jaws will pull together out of position.

When the jaws are thoroughly dry, they can be smoothed a bit with sandpaper to make a better appearance. Apply a couple of coats of shellac before painting: flat black, gold, or silver is especially effective. Screw the jaws to a stained plaque (Fig. 155). Add the angler's information in the lower center or lower right side of the trophy.

Letter Openers from Bills

A handsome letter opener—more a curio than a trophy—can be made from the bill of a sailfish or a small marlin. I collect all the bills I can and have fun producing letter openers which I

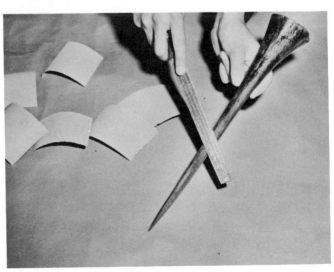

Fig. 156. Sailfish and marlin bills make unusual and attractive letter openers. File and sand the upper and lower (dorsal and ventral) sides.

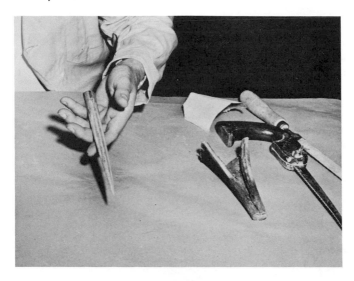

Fig. 157. Cut the base of the bill away from the solid front portion.
Polish and add a handle.

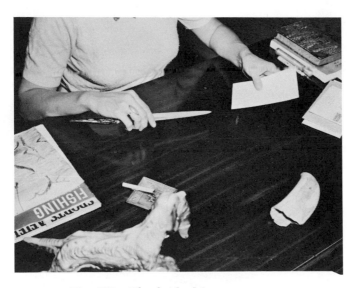

Fig. 158. The finished letter opener.

pass out as gifts to my friends. This type of letter opener is especially appreciated as an unusual conversation piece.

The process is simple. Cut about 12 inches off the end of the bill. Plan to have 8 inches as the blade of the opener and the remaining 4 inches to accommodate a handle. Use a file to wear down all the roughness of the bill, especially the rasp-like bottom side. Continue to file away, mostly on the top and bottom, until the bill takes on the appearance of a blade with its edges thin and smooth. Now go over the blade with two or three grades of sandpaper—from rough to very fine. When the opener takes on the smoothness of glass, polish it. This can be done with any type of abrasive polish such as rouge and an electrical buffing wheel. I get excellent results, however, by dipping a piece of cheesecloth into alcohol and dabbing it into whiting. Then it's a matter of rubbing it on, applying more alcohol and whiting, and rubbing some more.

File the hind 4 inches of the bill to a shape which will accommodate whatever handle you intend to put on it. My wife, Bo, found an interesting, small, silver umbrella handle in the shape of a duck's head complete with glass eyes and ivory bill at an antique shop that made a most attractive handle for a marlin-bill letter opener. I placed some liquid plastic into the metal end of the handle and pushed the handle end of the bill into it. I held it in position in a vise until the plastic set.

However, it is not necessary to hunt around in antique shops for an appropriate handle. If you are handy with a pen knife, carve one; or look for an old hunting-knife handle or a stag-horn handle which can be removed from a discarded kitchen carving set.

Five or 6 inches off a tine or prong of a deer's antler can be made into a beautiful handle. Simply drill a hole in the tine and glue the paper cutter in it.

9
Amateur Fish Museums

Amateur nature museums are surprisingly numerous. The urge
to collect things is strong within everyone. There are those
who collect books, stamps, antiques, neckties, deer antlers, cook-
ing recipes, photographs, bird lists, guns, tools, shrubs, fishing
tackle—one can go on indefinitely. Another strong urge in men
is to delve into things of nature; every week end of the year,
throughout the country, hundreds of thousands of people visit
museums of natural history. Combine the two—interest in
nature and the urge to collect—and a powerful force is born.
One of the best ways to satisfy this urge is to build an amateur
museum at home.

These home museums vary greatly. My attention has been
called to every degree of endeavor in this respect, from a shelf
covered with sea shells to entire rooms lined with glass cases
holding valuable collections of minerals. All summer camps
for children have a nature museum of some sort. Tourist stops
in hundreds of places around the country have museums as
attractions. Since I am a professional museum man, I tend to
examine these various amateur museums with a critical eye. I
find that the one great omission in nature museums is the lack
of fish exhibitions—this despite the fact that fishes and fishing
draw more popular interest than all the other amateur museum
subjects combined! I have scanned all available literature pertaining to fish preservation and exhibition, both technical and
popular, and find that fishes are either treated very lightly

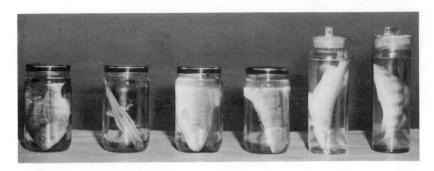

Fig. 159. Fishes preserved for display in a 10 per cent solution of Formalin (nine parts water, one part Formalin). *Left to right:* Bluegill, smelt, brook dace, sucker, pickerel, and perch.

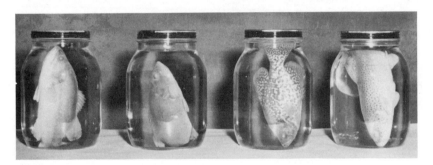

Fig. 160. Also in 10 per cent Formalin—largemouth bass, smallmouth bass, crappie, brown trout.

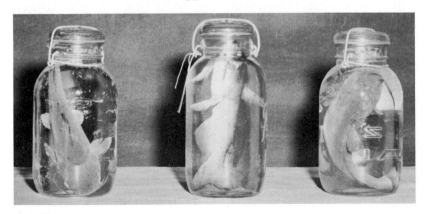

Fig. 161. White catfish, channel catfish, and black bullhead.

or ignored completely. No wonder amateur naturalists have omitted fishes in their museums—there has been no encouragement.

The collection and preservation of fishes for amateur museums in nearly every part of the country is easy. The actual collecting of specimens is fun, and the planning and execution of fish exhibits can be interesting and educational. The project is inexpensive. Every summer camp, school, boy-scout organization, and national park museum, regardless of the part of the country where it is situated, should have an exhibition of at least the local fishes.

As soon as the fish exhibit has been allotted a certain section in the nature museum—a room, cabin, tent, or any other type of shelter—the first thought that comes to mind is mounted fishes, and this is the point at which the fish exhibition idea is usually discarded! Mounted fishes are not necessary, though the camp or school class in crafts can be asked to join the project by making plaster casts of the local fishes as described previously. An easy, attractive, and interesting way of displaying fishes is to place them individually in a liquid solution in jars. But, let us start from the beginning.

Collecting the Fishes

Rod and Reel. First, and most important, the collection or exhibition must start with local fishes. Lakes, streams, brooks, ponds, brackish waters, and the seashore all have their share of interesting kinds. Of course the most obvious specimens will be fishes that are taken on rod and reel, so there is no problem in securing these. Make an effort to catch at least one specimen of all the known or common fishes. For example, when taking lake fishes include even catfish and eels because, as I will point out later, interesting exhibits can be formed with these also.

Seining. After all the rod and reel fishes have been collected, attention should be given to the lesser known types which can be taken by other methods. Indiscriminate seining or trapping of fishes, other than for bait, is prohibited by law in most fresh

waters of the United States. Nevertheless, all state fish and
game departments are cooperative when an educational project
is at hand. A responsible person can obtain such a state permit
to collect the fishes necessary for a school, camp, or boy-scout
project. Send a letter to the director of your state fish and game
or conservation department. In any event, the majority of
fishes that would make a good amateur museum collection can
be taken legally with rod and reel.

Seining is productive, and collecting in this manner is great
fun. Common minnow seines, available at most tackle dealers
in 6-, 10-, 12-, 15-foot lengths and 4- to 6-foot depths serve well.
A ¼-inch square is the usual size of the seine mesh. This type
of net has pieces of lead along the bottom and wooden floats on
the top. The ends of each side, top and bottom, are equipped
with ¼-inch rope extensions which should be tied, at each end,
to a broom handle or appropriate lengths of bamboo or tree
limbs which are fairly straight. Light-weight electrical conduit
pipe can be used also. The collectors manipulate and extend
the seine by means of these two handles.

Along the shallows of a lake or seashore, two men can do an
efficient job of seining. One works up close to the shoreline
while the other extends the seine out directly from shore, as far
as it is safe for him to progress. Both collectors then walk along
a short distance dragging the lead side of the seine along the
bottom. It is important that the seine hugs the bottom as it
goes along because fish will try to squirm under it and escape.
The seine should be kept at an angle which will facilitate its
progress through the water. However, do not drag the floats
under the surface.

Seining must be done at a fairly rapid pace. If progress is
slow the trapped fish will hit the seine and then quickly swim
along the length of it and escape at the outer end. After
going along for about 10 feet, the person working the deep end
of the seine should increase the speed to as fast as he can
progress—without falling into the water! The collector holding
the shore end of the seine will have to slacken his pace. In
other words, the seine is worked quickly and brought around

until the entire line of the seine is paralleled to shore. As the outer man approaches the shore, he must keep the seine taut; there should not be any belly in it. This is the point at which many fish escape. Both men must slide the lead side of the seine, still scraping the bottom, right up to the water's edge. Keep an eye on the float edge of the seine. Do not let it drag under the surface; it should be above and out of the water, or the fish will go right over it as they zoom around frantically when approaching shallow water at the shoreline. The whole action must be continuous.

Often the shore area contains obstructions which make it difficult for two men to scramble out while holding the seine taut with the trapped fish. In this case they should pull the seine out of the water, and both men should fold it in two lengthwise. Then they should walk toward each other folding the seine at arms length as they go along. In other words, the seine ends up like a bag with the fish in the bottom in the hands of one man.

When working a brook or a stream, the pools with fairly quiet waters are worked the same way as described above. In swift waters, however, a different technique is employed. Three men are required to do a good job. The seine is placed across the stream or brook so that a slight belly or trap is formed. The seine should be held at an angle to offer less resistance to the water. The float side of the seine can be a couple of feet out of the water. Check the position of the lead or bottom side so that it is not over boulders which would leave a space for fish to escape. Now the third man steps into the center of the water, about 10 or 15 feet upstream, and kicks over rocks, pebbles, and stones by dragging his feet along the bottom as he progresses as quickly as possible toward the stationary seine. Two or even three persons can do this for best results. All the small fishes, which were sheltered under and behind the stones etc., on the stream bed, will be carried by the current quickly downstream into the seine before they can regain their equilibrium and again scoot under a rock. When the stone kickers come close, the two men at the seine lift it up quickly with one motion. If the procedure is carried out properly, the collectors will be amazed at the amount of tiny fish life in each haul. Usually, the catch will consist of small minnow-like forms which have never been seen by the average fisherman.

Trapping. Some types of fishes will not strike a bait readily, or they live in water too deep to seine. For these, a trap can be employed. Occasionally, a regular minnow trap will do the

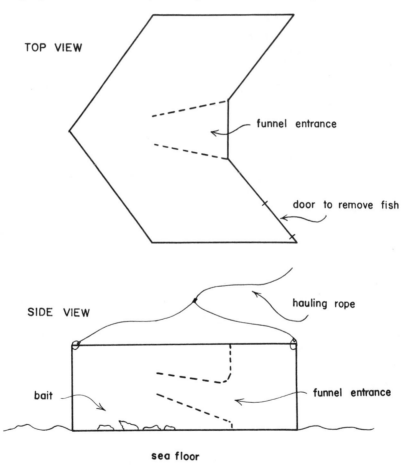

Fig. 162. Arrowhead-shaped fish pot used by fishermen in Bermuda, Puerto Rico, and other Caribbean islands. It may be constructed entirely of wire mesh.

job nicely, the kind that can be purchased at most tackle shops. Simply open the trap, drop in some bait such as fish heads or old pieces of meat, and let it stay in the water overnight.

In salt water I have experimented with different types of traps. I have placed them on the sea bottom around docks and bridge pilings, and I have set them from a rowboat in pro- ductive-looking areas in the vicinity of submerged rocks and reefs. I found that the arrow-shaped fish pot used in Bermuda, Puerto Rico, and other islands of the Caribbean was by far more successful than the funnel-shaped trap. Several of these traps can be constructed easily with ¾-inch mesh or chicken wire (Fig. 162). A hauling rope with a red-colored float on the one end is tied to the trap. The rope should be long enough so that it will not be submerged by high water. At one end of the trap, a 6- or 8-inch square opening is cut in the mesh and a wire door attached to it. When the trap is pulled out of the water, it can be so tipped that the fishes fall toward the door and can be re- moved easily. Also, new bait can be inserted. In salt water, bait which draws fishes is made up of clams and mussels with broken shells, old shells, fish heads, and old meat. Light- colored broken dishes placed in with the bait are an added attraction.

Fishery scientists supplement seining and trapping methods by other means—electrical shockers that stun the fish, and a poison, rotenone, which kills fishes by affecting their breathing apparatus. However, amateur collectors need not concern themselves with these methods of collecting.

Preserving the Fishes

Fishes up to the size of a largemouth bass, pickerel, trout, or bluefish can be preserved for display easily in formaldehyde or Formalin (Figs. 159 to 161). This chemical can be procured at any drug supply house. Your local druggist can help you. One quart will go a long way. The preserving solution is made with one part Formalin to nine parts water. Be sure to *read* the sec- tion on Formalin before working with it.

Professionals use the following method for optimum permanent preservation of fishes. The average specimen—5 to 10 inches—is kept in the 10 per cent solution of Formalin from two days to a week for adequate fixation. The specimen is removed from the Formalin and soaked in water for two or three days with at least a couple of changes of water. Then the fish is transferred to 70 per cent ethyl alcohol, or to isopropyl alcohol, which is better and cheaper. One change of alcohol is recommended before permanent storage. The reason why professionals remove the specimens from Formalin and place them in alcohol is that over a lengthy period of time the Formalin tends to harden soft parts and soften bony tissue. Also, alcohol specimens are easier to handle for study.

However, amateur museum developers can forget about the alcohol. It is expensive and not absolutely necessary. I have hundreds of specimens which have been kept in a weak Formalin solution for over twenty years, and they are just as good today for display purposes as the day they were first preserved.

The strength of the solution can be varied from the standard 10 per cent. Unusually large fishes (anything bigger than about a 5-pound bass) can be placed in eight parts water to one part Formalin, or very small specimens can be preserved in more dilute Formalin, fifteen to one. Generally, specimens over a few inches in length should have an incision along the abdomen so that the preserving solution can penetrate more easily into the insides (Fig. 163). Make the cut as high up on the side of the abdomen as possible. And the right side is usually chosen for the incision. This will leave the left side for the show side with no marks on it. Use a sharp knife; the incision should be at least half the length of the body cavity. Fish over 2½ or 3 pounds should have additional cuts deep into the flesh to facilitate penetration of the Formalin. This can be done from the outside. The specimen will make a neater display, however, if these cuts are made through the slits that were made in the body cavity. Or a fairly wide section can be removed as shown in Fig. 164. Cut long and deeply into the muscle mass on each side of the vertebral column (backbone).

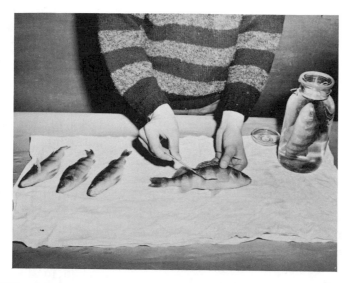

Fig. 163. Specimens over a few inches in length, such as these yellow perch, should have an incision along the abdomen so that the preserving solution (10 per cent Formalin) can penetrate more easily into the inside.

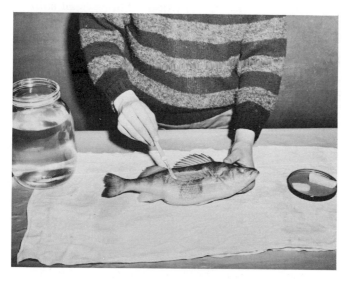

Fig. 164. In larger fishes, a fairly wide section of skin and meat can be removed to facilitate the entrance of Formalin.

If the specimens are to be stored permanently in Formalin and not alcohol, household borax should be added; it retards shrinkage, hardening of soft parts, and softening of bony material. To 1 quart of preserving solution add 1 level teaspoonful of borax. Also, if the specimens are to be displayed permanently in Formalin, it is a good idea (after a couple of weeks) to change the specimen into a new, clean solution of more dilute Formalin (about fifteen to one) to which household borax has been added.

Camp counselors, school teachers, scoutmasters, etc., who may desire to demonstrate the anatomy of Formalin-preserved fishes to their groups so that the fishes can be handled, should eliminate the objectionable fumes of Formalin in the following manner. The local druggist or the high-school chemistry teacher can supply 1,260 grams of $NaHSO_3$ (sodium bisulfite) and 840 grams of Na_2SO_3 (sodium sulfite). (There are 454 grams in a pound.) These salts are dissolved in tap water. Then enough water is added to make 5 gallons of solution. The Formalin specimens are rinsed in water before being immersed for a few minutes in this solution. Many specimens can be treated successfully in this bath before a new mixture is required. Do not allow the specimen to dry out in the course of demonstration. When it has served its purpose, it should be returned to the Formalin for storage.

Preserving in the Field

For the best results specimens should be dunked into the Formalin as soon as possible. Small specimens—up to the size of a 10-inch trout—should be placed in the can or jar of Formalin alive, as soon as collected. The fishes do not suffer; they are killed quickly, but they take in the preservative and extend their fins—all of which makes a better display specimen. Care should be used when placing the wiggling fish into the preservative receptacle. When the fish feels the initial sting of the Formalin, it will thrash around; and drops of Formalin may accidentally splash into the collector's eyes. If this happens, bathe the eyes *immediately* in clean water. However, if the cover of the container is held in one hand and clamped down as soon as the fish enters, there should be no difficulty. Obviously, do not attempt to insert a fish into a full jar of Formalin.

Scientists accustomed to working with Formalin may carry glass "Ball jars" during short collecting trips. In the field, however, the amateur should use some sort of nonbreakable receptacle such as a paint can which has a lid or one of the inexpensive plastic-type containers which come in all sorts of sizes and shapes. It is important that any receptacle used in the field be equipped with a lid which cannot be shaken off while traveling. A glass jar of Formalin can be a dangerous thing if broken by accident. When the specimens reach home or the laboratory, they should be rinsed in water to remove any foreign material adhering to them. Then their abdomens should be cut as previously described.

Jars for Specimen Display

Expensive jars are not necessary for display. Food stuffs of all types are packed in screw-top jars. Wide-mouth pickle jars are especially good for fish preservation and exhibition. Restaurants, delicatessens, school and camp kitchens, etc., discard large jars of all types. They are usually happy to cooperate in saving jars for you. Any fish can be displayed to greater advantage if it is placed alone in a jar. Situate the specimen against the glass in the jar so that it can be viewed easily. Fish inserted tail first are easier to remove, head first. Then cover the specimen with the Formalin solution.

A professional touch can be given to each jar by attaching a tag which gives information about the species of fish. Include common and scientific name, locality of capture, date, and name of the collectors. Scientists insert waterproof labels into the jars; waterproof ink is used on the labels. Also, the information on the label is supplemented by other, detailed facts which are entered in a catalog: type of water, vegetation, bottom, shore, distance from shore or stream width, depth of capture, water temperature, air temperature, current, tide, and time of day. Obviously, recording these facts is not necessary for amateur display specimens. However, I strongly recommend that camp counselors, scout leaders, and teachers meticulously employ this procedure with their students, for this presents an unusual opportunity to teach children to observe. And intelligent observation is the bases of every science.

But let's get back to the display jars. Regardless of the different sizes and shapes of the "store jars," the collection can be unified by painting all the jar tops one color. A bright color will detract from the specimens; paint them black.

Organization of Fish Exhibits

The display collection may contain many fine specimens, but it will lose most of its value if it is just a bunch of jars on a shelf. Here again, regardless of the persons involved or the type of the collection, scientific principles can be employed. Divide the fish into groups which will denote some type of classification that is easily understood: for example, a group of game fishes, a group of minnows, a group of bottom living fishes, etc. Or they may be divided into stream fishes and lake fishes, or fishes that can be taken by angling with a fly, those that will take spoons or plugs, and those that will take only bait.

Individual lessons in biology can be taught easily by intelligent display of preserved fishes. For example, have two jars side by side, one with a male trout and the other enclosing a female trout. Place the heads in the middle of the jars, against the glass, so that the smooth head and jaws of female can be compared easily with the angular, irregular jaws of the male. Cut the heads off a largemouth bass and a smallmouth bass and display them in individual jars. This exhibit will show that one is distinguished from the other by the length of the maxilla or upper lip which goes beyond the eye in the largemouth. This kind of exhibit is a lesson in observing anatomy more closely.

The fish exhibition in any amateur museum need not end with the collection of preserved local fishes. On the contrary, it should lay the groundwork for further exhibits. The many monthly outdoor magazines contain pictures of all types of fishes which can be cut out and pasted on large cardboards. Individual cardboards can read like this: BIG-GAME FISHES, OPEN OCEAN FISHES, SHORE FISHES, COMMERCIAL FOOD FISHES. Do not clutter up the poster-board exhibits (or any other for that matter) with long typewritten pages of reading matter. It is much better to letter the name under the fish with a colored crayon, then to one side add information that is easy to read from a distance:

THESE FISHES LIVE ONLY IN THE OPEN
OCEAN AND EAT ONLY OTHER FISHES
or
BOTTOM FISHES
EAT WORMS, SMALL CRABS, AND OTHER SMALL SEA ANIMALS

With preserved fishes to supply the professional look and a poster-picture display for treatment of other types of fishes, a fish section or an entire room or tent given to fishes can be more than a fine contribution to an amateur museum; it can be developed, with a guiding hand, into a most important teaching tool.

I have spent over twenty summers at boys camps as a camper, counselor, staff member, and nature instructor. The zoo and the nature museum are always the most popular projects in camp. During visiting hours on Sunday afternoons, the boys proudly show their parents the zoo and the museum. The exhibits which receive the most attention are the "question" type which can be changed every week. For example, the preserved catfish has a sign under it, "What are a catfish's whiskers used for?" The label under the eel reads, "Did you know that this eel came all the way from the deep waters of the Atlantic Ocean?" Under both captions is added "See the curators for answers." The curators are two or three members of the nature class who walk around, a bit proudly, with a small sign lettered on each peaked cap which reads CURATOR.

10

Fishes in Museums of Natural History

Within the last fifty years interest in fishes in the United States has boomed to unbelievable proportions. Fishing leads all other sports by a great majority in numbers of participants—one fifth of our total population, about thirty million persons of all races, religions, and ages. The varied academic subjects associated with fishery biology are taught in many of our best schools. Fishing and all it encompasses is big business; it is an important contribution to the economy of our country. Sport fishing alone is a multimillion dollar industry. And this great interest in fishes and fishing has not yet reached its peak.

Throughout the United States, museums of natural history attract hundreds of thousands of visitors annually. These throngs delight in viewing, at close hand, the vast range of exhibits associated with the natural sciences. Of course, the greatest attractions in any museum of natural history are the exhibits covering the vertebrates of the animal kingdom. Superlative halls of birds and mammals, and huge halls of paleontology which house the enormous skeletons of prehistoric animals, are common in museums. Then, is it not strange that despite the overwhelming popular and academic interest in fishes throughout the United States and other countries, the majority of museum fish exhibits and fish halls, to put it mildly, are a discredit to their respective institutions?

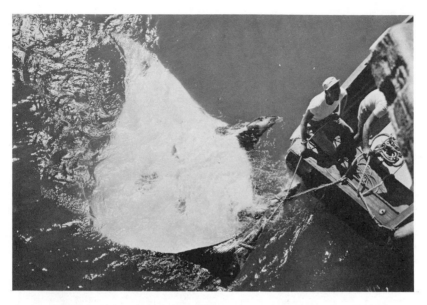

Fig. 165. After the battle off Cabo Blanco, Peru, which lasted for four hours, the giant manta is towed ashore.

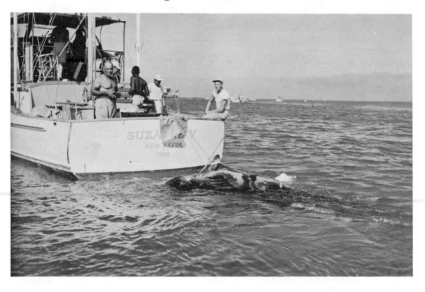

Fig. 166. The beast which was captured by harpoon weighed over 3,300 pounds and measured 18½ feet from wing tip to wing tip.

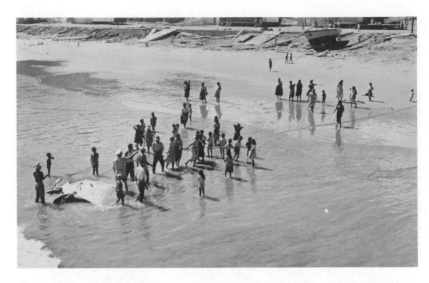

Fig. 167. It required just about the entire population of Cabo Blanco to drag the huge specimen ashore.

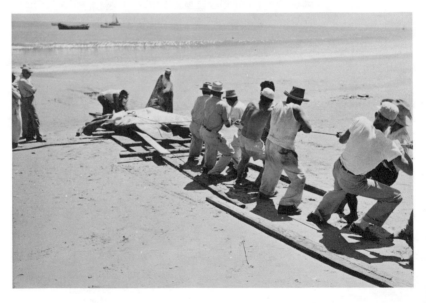

Fig. 168. Planks and rollers were placed under the manta. A rope was tied to a truck, and everyone pulled.

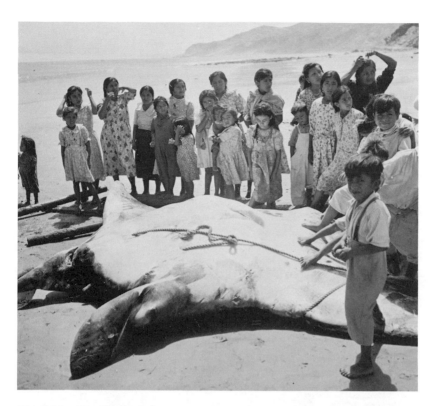

Fig. 169. We dragged the manta above the high-water mark. The local school was let out so that the children could see the manta.

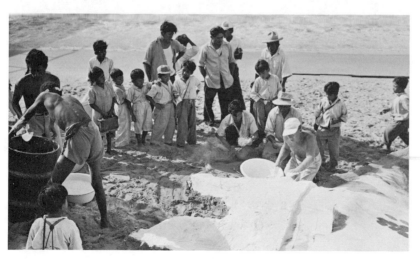

Fig. 170. The author finishing the first section of a four-piece mold.

175

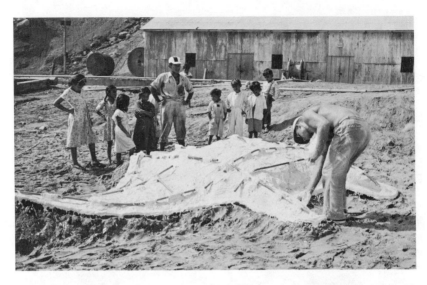

Fig. 171. Ten hours later the last reinforcing rod is attached to the mold.

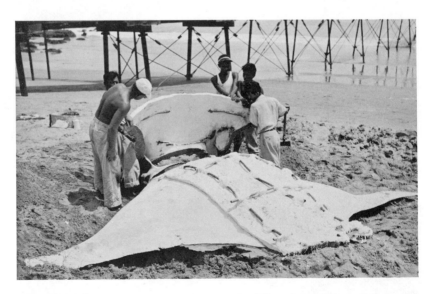

Fig. 172. The project was a great success. The wing sections of the mold have been taken off. Now the head portion is being removed. The individual sections were crated and transported to Yale University by ship.

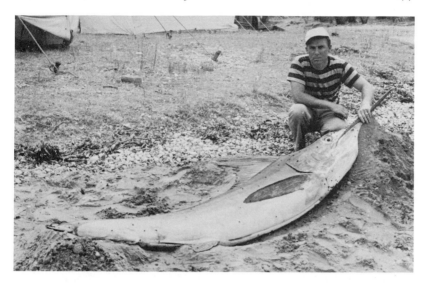

Fig. 173. To get away from stiff boardlike mounts, the important work is done in the field. Here a striped marlin is being readied to receive the plaster in molding. Note the graceful, natural curvature formed in the body. This effect is accomplished by propping up the head and tail sections with beach sand.

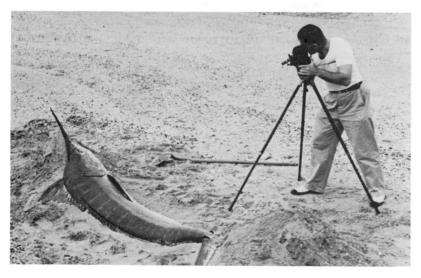

Fig. 174. A New Zealand photographer taking close-ups.

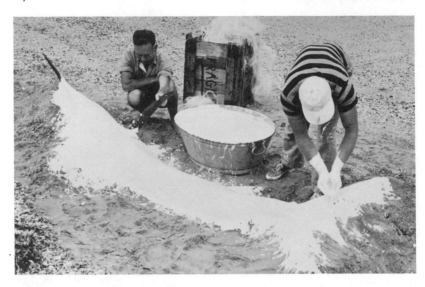

Fig. 175. The first or "splash" coat is applied. This step should be done in one uninterrupted operation.

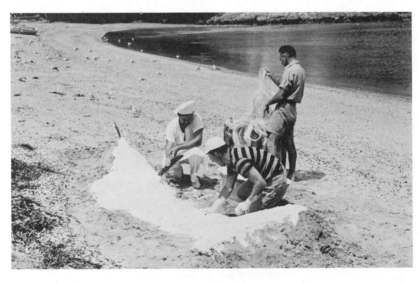

Fig. 176. The next coat of plaster is reinforced with sisal. Two assistants are required. In the field, local people usually are glad to help.

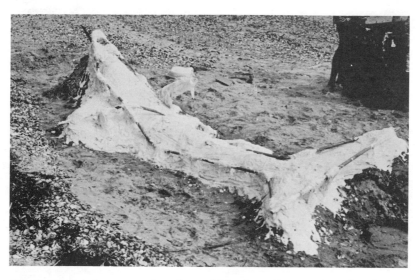

Fig. 177. It is important that the mold be braced or reinforced with pipe so that it will not crack during handling and transit.

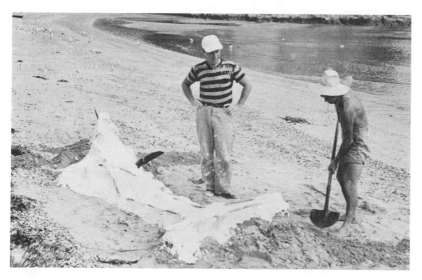

Fig. 178. After the mold has hardened, shovel out the sand from under the head and tail areas. It is easier to cut the pectoral fin away from the body instead of molding around it as shown above.

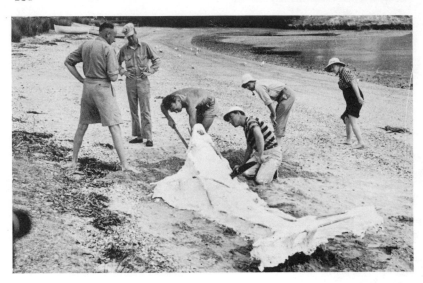

Fig. 179. Free the tail by pulling it down from the mold. Do the same to the head. Additional shoveling may be necessary.

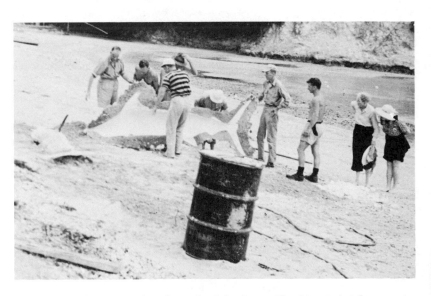

Fig. 180. When first taken from the fish, the mold is heavy (with water in the plaster) and requires able-bodied assistants to carry it.

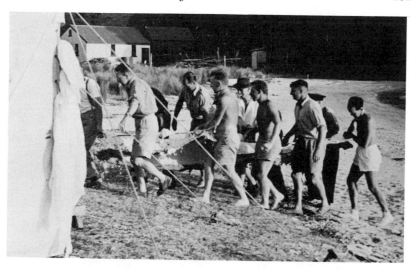

Fig. 181. It took an even dozen men to carry this mold of a big striped marlin into the shelter of the tent. The mold should be kept out of the rain so that it can dry and become lighter, and consequently easier to handle.

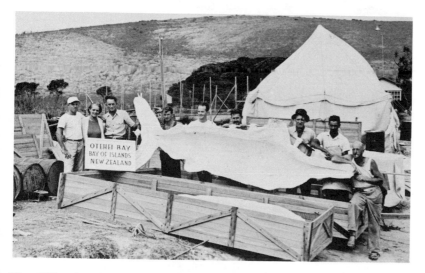

Fig. 182. A carpenter was hired to build these shipping crates. The author (left) stands with Mr. and Mrs. Buck Hassel of Otehei Bay. The other local folks were kind with their cooperation in handling the huge molds.

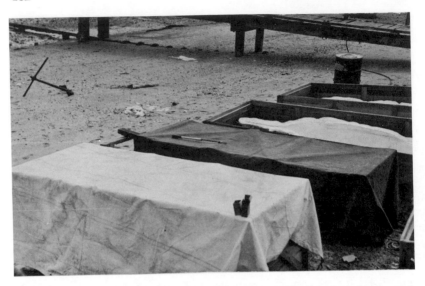

Fig. 183. The crates are protected from the rain and damp nights with canvas until shipped.

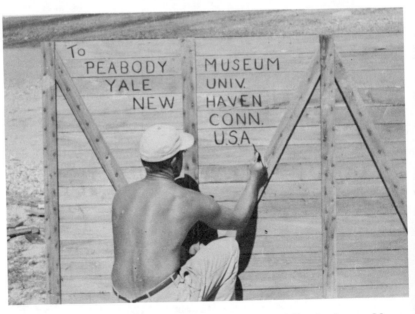

Fig. 184. The curator or preparator should personally check on addressing and arranging the shipment of molds to the museum.

History of Museum Preparation

The preservation of animals so that they can be displayed indefinitely is not a recent idea. A review of the history of museum exhibition portrays the gradual evolution of methods and results over the past several hundred years, from a crude beginning of "stuffed" specimens to the present magnificent works of art in great halls of famous museums.

It is interesting to investigate the origin of the early attempts at animal preservation. There are, of course, many examples of the cave man's crude use of animal skins; he formed them over mud and rocks to imitate live animals for ritual purposes. For the same reason the Egyptians, who pioneered the art of embalming, preserved animals in their entirety. One may search further and note that in Peru there is recorded the use of preserved bird skins for ornamental purposes as early as A.D. 1200. The Spanish conqueror of Mexico, Cortez, informs us that Montezuma, whom he dethroned, possessed robes covered with the skins of trogons and other birds of brilliant plumage. Unfortunately, history records these facts only because they are associated with the outstanding figures of the times. However, it may be safely assumed that there must have been "stuffed birds" in existence during a period when work with bird skins was so popular. Five centuries before Christ, Hanno, the Carthaginian navigator, collected gorilla skins which were preserved for generations. Actually, as far as it can be ascertained, this is the earliest recorded attempt to preserve an animal skin for a purpose other than ritual. One of the earliest recorded examples of an entire mammal mounted for museum exhibition occurred in Italy. A rhinoceros was "stuffed" for the museum of Ulysses Aldrovandus in Bologna in the sixteenth century. Later it was transferred to the Royal Museum of Vertebrates in Florence.

This is not the place for an extended thesis on the evolution of museum preparation and exhibition, but I have pursued the subject fully and followed the recorded word of improvements

by date and step by step. This research on museum development can be accomplished with satisfaction on bird and mammal mounting. But what about fish?

In contrast to developments in bird and mammal taxidermy,
tracing the history of fish mounting is a frustrating and fruitless
task. Why is the recorded word on the progress of the subject
so rare? Simply because the preservation and mounting of a
fish skin was always discouraging, never satisfactory. There
was no progress to record!

The date of an early attempt at fish mounting comes from an
unexpected source, from Shakespeare, *Romeo and Juliet*, Act V,
which appeared in 1596, gives us a clue:

> I do remember an apothecary,—
> And hereabouts he dwells, which late I noted
> In tatter'd weeds, with overwhelming brows,
> Culling of simples; meagre were his looks;
> Sharp misery had worn him to the bones:
> And in his needy shop a tortoise hung,
> An alligator stuff'd and other skins
> Of ill-shaped fishes.

The extract not only gives a date for the early presence of
fish taxidermy but also accentuates the fact that centuries have
passed and still many of our best museums continue to display
"ill-shaped fishes." Not much progress!

I have been fortunate in being able to visit the best museums
of natural history in the United States, Canada, England,
France, Belgium, New Zealand, Hawaii, India, South America,
and Africa. To my knowledge there is not one which has a
hall of fishes that compares in standard to the great halls of
birds, mammals, or vertebrate paleontology in many museums
today.

There are several reasons why this is so. The preparation
of fishes for museum exhibition was difficult. Mammals can be
modeled to perfection; their skins are preserved indefinitely
by tanning, and coloration is no problem since it is naturally
retained. The feathers of mounted birds cover skin damage
and built-up anatomical blunders; at least most of the museum

birds of today look respectable. Most of the museum fish specimens are mounted skins, which are almost invariably monstrosities. A mounted fish skin eventually splits and oozes
grease; the fins crack; and the head shrinks to distortion, and
attempts to rebuild it with wax are unsatisfactory. Some
museums use models. Most of these models are rigid and have
no character; their fins are flat and without expression, cut from
Celluloid or other material. And nearly all of the fishes are
painted by persons who have never seen the specimens alive.

Criteria for Museum Fish Mounts

Today there is no excuse for poor fish mounting and poor fish
exhibition. True colors of fishes are easily recorded with today's variety of wonderful color films. The greatest boon to the
art of fish displays was the advent of plastics and other synthetic
materials. Any fish can be molded in plaster and cast accurately
in durable artificial materials. Transportation of working materials to the field of operations and return of plaster molds is
no longer an obstacle.

But, let's start from the beginning. I would like to speak to
museum curators, preparators, and commercial taxidermists
like a "Dutch uncle." Before delving into the mechanics of
producing accurate, durable, lifelike reproductions of fishes in
synthetics, it is important to know what a live fish really looks
like. This is not a ridiculous statement, for I'm surprised to see
that when detail of fish anatomy is involved, even some trained
scientists fail to observe intelligently. I would like to suggest a
few pointers for scientists and technicians to keep in mind when
pleasing, accurate reproductions are desired.

1. *Body.* The most common fault found in fish mounts, and
one that preparators and commercial taxidermists insist on
promulgating, is the contorted body. These gentlemen think
that to twist a fish's body dorso-ventrally—from top-side to
bottom-side—depicts "action." No such thing. The fish is no
longer a delight to look at; it has its back broken and its curva-

tures are crippled. The fish appears to be in agony. Whenever
I see such a mount, I have a feeling that I should hit it over the
head with a club to stop its misery.

Watch a fish in the water; its body movements are from side
to side, not from top to bottom. Look at an action photograph
of a hooked fish (one that has not been faked); again, the body
is bent laterally. Next time you see a movie of a marlin or of
any other fish jumping, note that its head and tail swing from

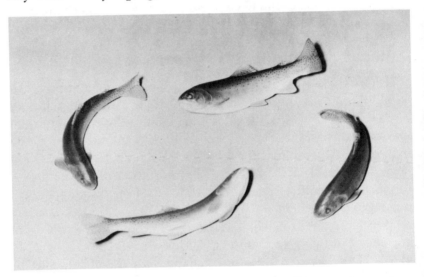

Fig. 185. The natural curvatures of a fish's body are lateral, that is, from
side to side as shown above—not twisted up and down into grotesque forms.

side to side, not up and down. In other words, it is physically
impossible for a game fish to bend into violent curves which
bring its head and tail down or up at extreme angles. The
anatomy of the fish will not permit it. A *slight* downward or
upward bend in the tail region is fine, and any mount will have
plenty of action by turning its head or tail, or both, slightly away
from the wall (Fig. 185).

2. *Fins.* Next to the body itself, the fins are the most notice-
able pieces of anatomy on a fish. With the proper angulation
and curvature placed in the fins, any type of action desired in

a mount can be accentuated. But for heavens sake, *do not stretch the fins* to their extreme width and *do not force them away from the body.*

It is practically impossible to find a mount that does not have its fins dried flat, stretched to their fullest and away from the body. The fish appears to be frozen in fright—like a "funny cartoon" which shows a man's hair standing straight up when he sees a ghost. Again, think. When a fish is stationary or swimming, its fins are undulating in movement; there are smooth curves within the fins which do not stretch violently. The fins do not open and close like a Japanese fan. Form pleasing curves in the fins, whether you dry them in position or reproduce them in plastic. For example, you can portray a mount, swimming swiftly, by positioning the fins backward, especially the dorsal fins. Fishes use their tails and body for propelling themselves through the water. The fins are mostly stabilizers in one respect or another.

3. *Mouth.* Here again, the tendency is to exaggerate. The open mouth is forced wide beyond all reasonable action. This fault is especially apparent in the largemouth bass. Have you ever seen a mount of this species which did not have its mouth pulled wide into distortion? If you have it's a rarity. Why do taxidermists stretch a fish's mouth into ugliness? Wouldn't it be more pleasing to open a mouth partially? Every mounted largemouth bass I have seen looked worse than if it were trying to regurgitate a big bullfrog and failing in the attempt. We know it is a largemouth bass because the end of the maxilla (upper lip) reaches backward beyond the eye, not because its mouth has been stretched to appear like the opening of a sewer-pipe.

4. *Eye.* The eye of a mounted fish is nearly always too large, and it is easy to find out why. Next time you see a fresh fish, observe its eye closely. Notice that the eye is in a ball that fits into a socket. Also note that the extreme width all around the eye is not as wide in diameter as the eye socket. A taxidermist removes the eyeball, and replaces it with a glass

eye that fits exactly into the entire socket and which, of course, is much bigger than the original eye. To do a good job on the eye of a mounted fish, a portion of the eyeball should be indicated and the width of the eye proper, measured. A glass eye of the same size should be inserted.

5. *Color.* It is more difficult to criticize the paint job of a mounted fish. First, all species of fishes go through different shades of intensities of coloration at one time or another. Often two specimens of the same type of fish, inhabiting waters only a few miles apart, will be different in coloration. If an angler is accustomed to fishing in one area, he may consider a mount of the same species of fish, taken from another area, as being inaccurately painted. Second, a mounted fish is not easy to paint. Anyone expecting to do a professional job must have natural ability plus accurate knowledge of the coloration of the live fish.

One of the most important steps in painting mounted fishes is to secure color transparencies of the fish while it is alive or as soon as it is dragged out of the water. The photos must be supplemented by color notes. Unless the artist has confidence in his knowledge of the subject, the mount will be inferior. Read the suggestions for techniques of recording color of the specimen in the field in Chapter 1 and techniques of painting in Chapter 5.

Museum Field Work

Museums of the world have had a more or less standard procedure in caring for fishes which were to be used for display. Fishes taken in distant areas were skinned, packed in salt, and sent to the museum. If the specimens were not too large and taken closer to home, they were packed in ice and shipped. Some museums working directly in the field made molds of a few large fish such as sharks.

However, the only method that will produce superior mounts is to make plaster molds of all fishes as soon as they can be

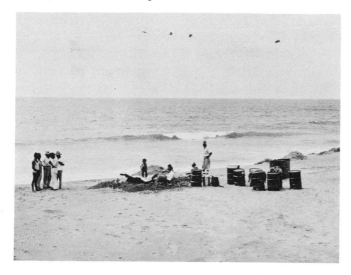

Fig. 186. The museum's field men must arrive a few days in advance to set up a beach area for working. Fresh water has to be brought down to fill a couple of barrels. The plaster and all working equipment must be there also. Check to see whether or not the natives will pilfer your supplies when left unguarded at night.

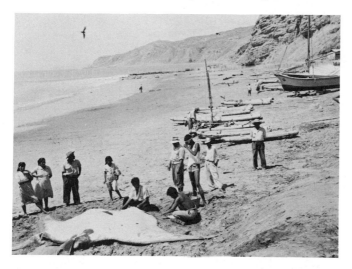

Fig. 187. Clean sand, fairly free of debris and shells, should be chosen for the working area. The sand is soaked with water and used for a shelf around the body where necessary, or to prop up portions of the specimen.

brought ashore. Second best is to freeze the fish as soon as possible (see Chapter 1). Every museum mount should be cast in a durable synthetic. Even skins of fishes that are difficult to obtain should never be mounted. Instead, the skin should be filled and modeled as accurately as possible to its former shape. A mold is made of it and then cast in one of the new plastic-like materials. Incidentally, this is also an excellent way to save old mounts of skin specimens. Model the shrunken head, lips, etc., with modeling clay; and then proceed with the molding as if the fish were a fresh specimen.

Foreign Shipping, Materials, and Customs. The entire procedure of molding fish in the field is not as difficult as it may appear. I have made molds of fishes, varying in size from a ½-pound snapper to a manta ray weighing 3,300 pounds, on distant beaches around the world, in Africa, Alaska, New Zealand, South America, etc. Every mold arrived in excellent condition at Yale University. Since my methods have evolved over the years—mostly by trial and tribulation—I am sure that curators, preparators, and others doing this type of field work will find the following information of unusual value.

If the expedition is to take place outside the shores of the United States, be sure to secure all of the supplies here. Ship them by freighter to their destination. I purchased plaster of Paris, of a foreign make, in another country and regretted it. The plaster was inferior, and I had a bad time trying to produce first-class molds. Only No. 1 molding plaster should be used. I have experienced this type of exasperation several times; therefore, regardless of what fine reports I may receive concerning availability of supplies in remote areas, I disregard them and ship plaster, sisal, pipe, Formalin, tools, wire—everything. Sometimes the heavy material such as plaster can be purchased and shipped from a point closer to its port of embarkation, but this procedure also presents complications.

Through correspondence, or better yet through an agent, make contact with customs officials at the point of arrival in the foreign country and with the customs people in the United

States, where the returning materials will arrive. To demonstrate the necessity of checking well in advance with customs in this country, I relate the following experience. During an expedition to Africa, I shipped out 3,300 pounds of plaster. But, when the plaster returned to this country, in the form of fish molds, the trouble began. Some of the customs people in-

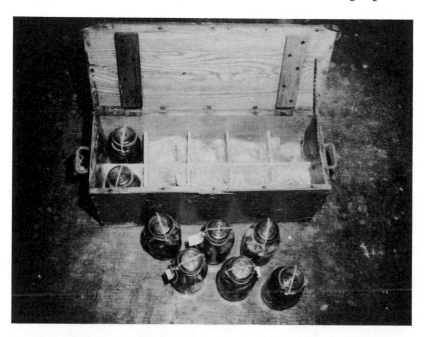

Fig. 188. Formalin can be shipped safely for long distances provided it is packed properly. Build individual compartments, as shown above, and pack sisal or excelsior on the bottom, top, and around the jars.

sisted that Yale University pay a duty on the molds (which would have been considerable with a return of over thirty molds of all sizes). The customs officials could not understand that the plaster was the same material which left the country—only in a different form. After weeks of correspondence and trips to New York, everything was finally untangled. Much time can be saved and wear and tear on the nervous system avoided if you make previous contact. However, be sure to get everything in writing; keep a file on all these transactions. Ship the materials months in advance. It is a rare freighter that departs and arrives on time, and be sure there is a capable agent at the other end to store supplies and equipment until an expedition member can take over.

Do not arrive "cold turkey," so to speak, and expect to put in a good day's work on the beach. If possible, plan to come a week or so early to prepare the work area, etc. It is even more important to use that time to advantage in gradual acclimation to the sun. I have worked all day, many times, on beaches near the equator where there was not a cloud in the sky; and temperatures hovered at the 100-degree mark. Yet I felt no ill effects, simply because I had exposed myself to the sun gradually for longer periods of time, over a week or so, before working on the beach.

Plaster of Paris should be packed according to distances involved, length of time in the field, facilities for transportation, etc. For example, if the expedition will be in the field for several months and many fishes are to be collected, I advise shipment of the plaster in 30-gallon drums, which will weigh 220 pounds each when filled with plaster. Specify "export type," provided with rubber gaskets and convenient lock-type covers. I shipped fifteen of these drums to Africa.

However, wherever possible it is more advantageous to ship the plaster in 5-gallon pails, available at most paint-distributing concerns. These pails are provided with metal handles and wooden grips which make the plaster easy to handle in the field. The lids are equipped with metal extensions which close the pail snugly when bent down, and rubber gaskets are included.

The pails are excellent as receptacles for returning Formalin specimens. After the specimens have been preserved thoroughly in Formalin, they can be packed in wet cheesecloth without being sent in Formalin. The pails will be in no danger of leaking Formalin, they will be much lighter in weight for shipping, and the specimens will not be harmed. For additional protection and moisture, I prefer to place wet sisal (other material can be used) around the specimens so that they will not damage one another during transit.

Each pail filled with plaster weighs close to 40 pounds. I usually pack four to a crate for shipment. During one expedition to South America, we had one boat sailing from Connecticut; therefore, I simply trucked the pails uncrated to the dock and loaded them on—fifty pails.

Amount of Plaster per Fish. For a collecting expedition to Alaska, I shipped sixteen pails of plaster packed in four crates. This was enough to mold three big salmon (35 to 40 inches, up to 52 pounds), two medium salmon (20 to 30 inches), two rainbows (30 inches each, two sheefish or inconnu (24 inches each), one grayling, one northern pike, one dolly varden or Arctic char, and one mackinaw or lake trout. A 45-inch or a 45-pound fish will require approximately one 5-gallon pail of plaster per side, or two pails for the fish.

As a further example of amounts of plaster per type of fish, the following specimens are some that I collected in the Bahamas: 7½-pound barracuda—40 pounds plaster or one pail; 16 pound—Nassau grouper—60 pounds plaster or one and a half pails; 5-pound blackfin tuna—40 pounds plaster or one pail; 36-pound amberjack—80 pounds of plaster or two pails.

I have enumerated the above as a rough guide. If one knows the type and number of fishes to be collected, the amount of plaster to be used can be ascertained fairly well. Always take a few extra cans. No. 1 Red Circle molding plaster comes in 100-pound bags. I have the bags sent to the museum laboratories where the plaster is transferred to the 5-gallon pails and crated. Three 5-gallon pails will accommodate a 100-pound bag of plaster with room to spare.

Water Supply. Fresh water is necessary to mix the plaster. When molding fresh water fishes, there is no problem. However, salt water expeditions require a makeshift laboratory on the beach with a supply of fresh water handy (another reason for early arrival on the scene). This is the way I do it. Two empty barrels or oil drums are secured and placed near the spot where the fish are to be molded. Pick a spot which harbors clean sand, with no excess of pebbles and shells. I always correspond with a contact man in advance concerning this type or problem, because a receptacle of this sort may be difficult to produce at short notice in a primitive area. Then I hire two or three natives and form a bucket brigade to fill the drums with fresh water. Or I may make arrangements to have the water trucked to the beach. Use this water to mix plaster, but have your native helpers run to salt water, which should be only a short distance away, and clean the plaster out of the pans in the surf. A scrub brush or a handful of sisal will facilitate removal of the plaster that is beginning to set. With a bit of joshing and an approving word now and then, I find that natives develop easily and quickly into valuable assistants.

Mold Reinforcement. In the field I always reinforce the mold. After the first or "splash" coat covers the fish, I apply another layer of plaster which has been strengthened with sisal. The sisal is torn or pulled away from the bale in convenient handfuls, dipped in the plaster so that it is thoroughly saturated, and carefully placed along the mold until the entire fish and the built-up shelf around it are covered. Sisal or tow is a strong hemp or fiber obtained from plants. I always have the sisal ready, that is, torn from the bale in small chunks, before mixing the plaster.

A two-piece mold is made of fishes up to about the size of a 75-pound specimen, or up to the point where fish and mold can be turned over to work the other side. However, fishes such as bluefin tuna, marlin, or sailfish have to be produced with a one-side or one-piece mold. Usually, it is possible to apply the plaster beyond the mid-line of the belly and head because the body of the soft fish can be removed, with some manipulation, from the mold. In the laboratory, a mold that continues beyond the mid-line of the back and belly can be chipped away to facilitate removal of the cast from it. When such a cast is exhibited, it will appear as a whole fish.

The mold is further reinforced with pipe. Conduit pipe is

ideal for the purpose. This pipe is strong but light in weight and can be cut easily with an ordinary hack saw. Also, it can be bent without trouble to fit roughly into the outside contours of the mold. The pipe is attached to the mold by spots of sisal dipped in plaster, in three or four places along each piece. Both sides of the mold are treated in this manner.

When the mold has set and the fish removed, the halves are placed together and tied with a piece of strong wire at each end. A mold of this type is surprisingly strong, but do not give it unnecessary abuse.

Crating Molds. A local carpenter should be employed to start crating the molds before the expedition has terminated because the procedure requires time and supervision. If two or three small molds are packed in one crate, they should be supported with wooden crossbars and wedges so that no damage occurs from contact between them during shipment.

Allow the molds to dry out as much as possible in the open air or in a shelter which has its windows or doors open during the day. In British Guiana, where it rained almost every night during our stay, I had my native assistants on a schedule, carrying the molds into the protection of a shanty toward night-fall. They returned them outdoors, to the sunshine, in the morning. Molds lose a great deal of weight when the moisture leaves them; dry molds are not only easier to handle but the shipping bill will be much less. Air freight, of course, is charged by weight. Cargo vessels, according to their shipping formulas, usually charge by whatever is greater—the size of the crate or its weight.

Setting the Fish for Molding. When preparing the fish for molding, natural turns and twists can be easily incorporated into the body by shoveling sand into strategic places under the fish. Producing a good mold is a mechanical affair; anyone who has the ability to work with his hands and who does not mind working like a dog under uncomfortable conditions can learn to construct them in the field. However, manipulating the fish into correct position for molding is another thing and requires some knowledge of fishes plus an artistic eye. Of course, in the case of a specific fish for a specific exhibit, the fish would have to be molded according to preset plans by the curator. If the curator is not in the field, the preparator should be armed with some sketches and concise notes as to the position the

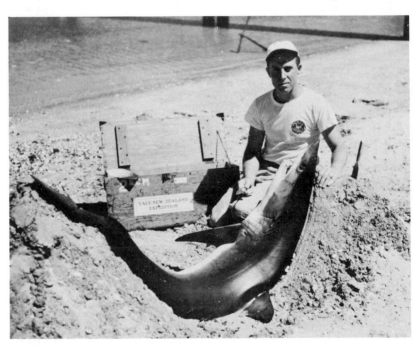

Fig. 189. Spectacular but accurate curvatures can be obtained in the mount. The mako shark above was molded in this position on the beach soon after it was caught.

various mounts are to take. Aside from not disintegrating in exhibition cases, the other great advantage of producing museum mounts from molds is that lifelike and true-to-form specimens can be produced.

Fins. Do not waste precious time in the field with tasks which can be accomplished in the museum. For example, I do not mold the pectoral and ventral fins on the spot; instead, I

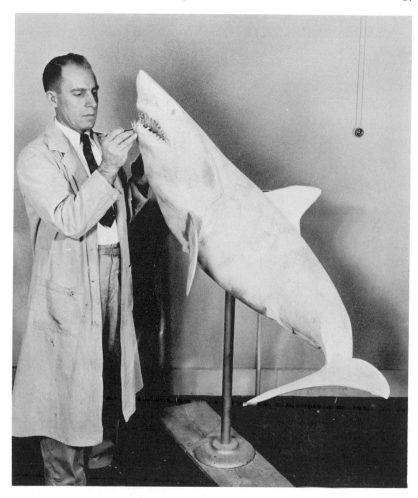

Fig. 190. The author is finishing the cast of the same shark in the museum laboratory.

cut them from the body with scissors or hack saw. (Do not cut so close as to remove a piece of body skin; otherwise, fluids will ooze out and prevent the plaster from setting in the area around it.) Then, I spread and tack the fins on pieces of wood and place them in a pan of 10 per cent Formalin so that they float, fins down. After the fins have been preserved in position, a day or two, I remove them from the wood, wrap them in cheese-cloth, add a tag, and then insert them in a bucket of Formalin until time for shipment. Incidentally, I usually preserve heads and other fins also. They are often invaluable for reference points in finishing the cast. Shark jaws, barracuda heads, and any other head which contains prominent dentition, which has to be removed from the original head and inserted into the head of the mount, should also be preserved.

Big-Game Fishes

For best results the mold should be made as soon as possible after the fish is caught. However, big-game fishing boats are usually too far out to sea to return immediately with a speci-men. Also, nothing would be gained if the anglers did return at mid-day rather than toward evening. A full, uninterrupted day is required to construct a mold of a large fish such as a marlin.

When the fish is removed from the boat, it should be placed on the dock, cleaned with buckets of water, and then wrapped with a double layer of potato sacks which have been saturated with water. If the weather is unusually warm, the abdomen can be injected with a 10 per cent solution of Formalin to prevent undue spoilage overnight. Buckets of water should be thrown over the wrapped fish again before retiring. Of course, if a large ice plant is handy, that is where the fish should be stored overnight.

Never leave the specimen in the water tied to the dock. Not only will the action of the sea damage the fish against the pil-ings, but decomposition will set in faster. Also, sea life that is active at night may chew on the specimen. If the fish is not covered with wet sacks overnight, it will shrink and shrivel and be practically worthless for a good mold in the morning. Arise as soon as the sun breaks the horizon and try to get the plaster on the fish in the cool of the morning.

If the curator or preparator is not a fisherman, he should, none the less, be aboard the fishing craft every possible moment that she is working out at sea. To be aboard to observe fishes in action is one of the most important parts of the job. Ideas for exhibition displays will be gained, and color photography of the live specimens, plus notes, will be possible. Last, but not least, the specimens can be cared for aboard the craft— and it is necessary regardless of the size of the fish. Small fishes should be wrapped in wet sacks and placed in the bait box. Large fishes that lie in the cockpit also have to be covered with wet burlap and occasionally wetted down with buckets of salt water. A specimen exposed to the sun and wind can be ruined in a short time.

One point to keep in mind—you may instruct the captain or mate to look after the specimen, and in all good faith he will agree to do so. However, as every angler knows, the captain and mate have their hands full, looking for fish, rigging baits, handling the boat, gaffing the fish, etc. Therefore, the specimen will not receive any attention once it is on the deck of the boat, regardless of how important it is to the museum. Furthermore, it is unfair to ask a boat crew to look after specimens. In any event the preparator or curator, who has an opportunity to discuss fish with experienced anglers, will be that much more valuable to the institution that employs him.

Obviously, I have omitted the step-by-step methods of the entire procedure of molding and casting because it is treated in detail in Chapters 2 and 3.

11
Repairing Fish Mounts

Although it is usually only the broken fins that require attention on a mounted fish, it is possible to do a major repair job on any part of the trophy. Skin mounts always need repair after being up on the wall, even though they may not be damaged from force. When the skin shrinks it cracks; grease will ooze at the base of the fins and tail. If the fins are artificial but the body skin original, a space will develop where they join. A cast of a fish, regardless of the kind of medium, will demand least attention over the years. As a matter of fact, a cast requires repairing only when physical damage occurs.

Fins

Fins with pieces broken off should be removed entirely and replaced with a new set. If the trophy is a skin mount, obtain fins from another fish, position them between two pieces of paper board, and keep together with paper clips until dry. The bases to accommodate the fins on the mount will have to be cut or drilled out. Wrap a thin layer of cotton, more if necessary, around the base of the fin and dip it into a good glue. The drilled hole in the mount may also require cotton dipped in glue. Brace the fin in position until the glue has set. If the mount has a wooden body, a few brads will hold the fin; but remove the brads when the glue has set. The cracks where the fin meets the body may be filled in with melted beeswax. The wax can be smoothed with a hot tool or an electrical pencil which is available at art shops. Apply a thin coat of shellac to the repaired area before painting.

If the fins or the tail are cracked between the rays and otherwise not damaged severely, they can be brought back to look normal by reinforcing them with cheesecloth and tissue paper. On the backside of the tail or fin, glue a piece of cheesecloth of the right shape. On the show side, glue a single sheet of tissue paper cut to the appropriate size. The fins and tail make a better appearance if their hind edges (where the rays branch out) are irregular. Therefore, arrange the ragged edges (tear, if necessary) of the cheesecloth and the paper so that they will meet with the irregular edges of the fins. Use a glue with some glycerin in it for flexibility (formula No. 7). When the glue has set, cut the excess cloth and paper away from the sides of the fin. A pair of scissors will do it. Shellac the repaired fins before painting. Torn or split fins can be repaired also by painting them, when thoroughly dry, with liquid Celluloid, on both sides. Place a piece of tissue paper on the backside and paint over it with more Celluloid. White shellac may be substituted if liquid Celluloid is unobtainable. Incidentally, this procedure may be used to reinforce the tail and fins of a freshly mounted fish after the fins have dried.

Any damaged fins on a plastic mount should also be replaced with new ones. Cut the fin off close to the body with a band saw or a hack saw. Use a drill to cut through the body of the mount for the fin base. Cast the fins and anchor them as described in Chapter 3. Fins cast in plastic can be used to replace damaged fins on any type of fish mount.

Head

The head of a skin mount will shrink. If it was not brought out to its original contours with wax (by the original taxidermist), it should be done. If the head has been waxed upon the original mounting and is cracked, do not attempt to patch it. Instead, dig and scrape away all of the old wax and remodel with fresh wax. Place a piece of beeswax in a double boiler. When it melts apply the wax to the head with a brush. When enough wax has been placed on the head, work it into shape by scraping a knife over the high spots. With a sharp tool carve in the necessary lines around the gills, lips, etc. Rub down the head with cheesecloth dipped in turpentine to smooth the head. Apply a thin coat of shellac over the waxed head before painting.

Body

Often, the scales on a skin mount will lift. In order to remedy the situation, it is necessary to remove the paint. Apply a standard type of paint remover until the paint is soft, and then wipe it off with a rag. Place some wet cloths over the scales until they soften and return to their normal position. Wipe the excess moisture off the fish and then brush on a thin coat of glue. When the glue has dried thoroughly, coat the entire fish with shellac (thinned 50–50 with alcohol) before painting (see Chapter 5). If the mount does not have too heavy a layer of paint, it will not be necessary to use paint remover. Scales will soften quickly if moisture is applied to the underside of the up-turned scales.

If the body skin is cracked, it should be glued back to the mannequin with a good contact cement. If there is a slight separation where the crack occurred, it can be filled in with melted beeswax. Scrape away the excess wax when it cools and then brush on the shellac before painting.

The inside of the mouth, if open, usually requires additional attention. Dig away all old wax; apply fresh beeswax (brushed on hot and melted); model into the desired shape with scraping tools and a hot iron; smooth with a cloth and turpentine; apply shellac before painting.

It is usually better to give the mount an entirely new paint job rather than attempt to patch up areas. Paint fades, and it is difficult to match an old paint job with fresh paint.

12

Materials and Formulas

In the old days taxidermy and museum preparation incorporated all kinds of formulas and mixtures, and most of them were secrets well guarded by the individuals using them. Today a fresher attitude is taken, at least in museums of natural history, and information pertaining to any part of museum preparation is gladly given. Also, there is less need for formulas and mixtures concocted in the laboratory. Today there is an amazing array of easily obtainable, inexpensive, durable materials which are a great boon to anyone interested in taxidermy, museum preparation, amateur museums, or fish mounting.

Furthermore, there is no need for long, impressive lists of "official tools" required for doing the work; this is especially true in producing fish mounts and other fish trophies. Discarded pots and pans, old kitchen spoons and dull knives, sharp pen knives, scissors, and "five and dime" spatulas are the type of "fancy tools" required. The other tools which may be necessary are the common saw, file, hammer, pliers, etc.

The different materials needed for constructing fish mounts can be purchased at local stores which deal in hardware, drugs, chemicals, paints, laboratory supplies, and mason supplies. Glass eyes, tow or sisal, and other specific materials can be obtained from one of many taxidermy supply houses advertised under "Taxidermy" in outdoor magazines. Therefore, I am listing only those materials that would require some trouble to locate. Also, I have kept the formulas down to a minimum and elaborated only wherever necessary.

Plaster of Paris

Plaster of Paris should be Grade "A" or "Number 1" molding plaster. It is inexpensive and is packed in 100-pound bags; procurable at most mason supply houses and occasionally lumber companies carry it. Art shops may have information as to where molding plaster may be purchased.

Sisal

Also called tow, hemp, sisal grass, or sisal hemp, sisal is a fine, strong, tough fiber which is obtained from the leaves of certain plants. If small quantities are needed, the best procedure would be to purchase it from a taxidermy supply house. If larger quantities are desired, however, sisal can be obtained by the bale from the Atlantic Excelsior Company, Inc., New York, New York. This company calls it "machine compressed manila casting fiber." A compressed bale will supply an amazing amount of casting fiber.

Woven Glass

Woven glass, filter cloth, or glass fiber cloth may be obtained in different mesh styles. For large fishes I prefer Style No. G-211; and for smaller fishes I use Style No. 210, which has a smaller mesh. The National Filter Media Corporation sells it. They are located at New Haven, Connecticut and at Salt Lake City, Utah. The style numbers may change. I would advise that you ask for some sample pieces and prices before ordering. It is sold by the yard.

Conduit Pipe

I have found that an excellent reinforcement for plaster molds, especially in the field, is thin wall conduit pipe (⅝-inch inside diameter). It is obtainable at electrical supply houses and comes in 10-foot lengths.

For shipping to distant areas, I cut it into 5-foot lengths and bind the pieces together into packages which can be handled easily. Then I wrap the individual bunches of pipe with burlap sacks. Be sure to insert each end of the package into a sack so that the individual pieces of pipe will not slip out.

Plastics and Resins

There are a wide variety of synthetic or plastic-like materials on the market today which can be used for casting, and anyone interested may find it worthwhile to experiment. A search into the advertising section of telephone directories will produce names and addresses of companies dealing in plastics and resins. Write to them for information concerning self-setting plastics.

Nearly all boat supply dealers carry polyester resins. These resins, combined with Fiberglas, are used extensively for repairing and reinforcing boat hulls. The same resins—usually packaged in gallon containers—are also excellent for producing casts of fishes. The resin, when mixed with a small amount of "hardener" or "activator" in a separate container, will set hard in about 20 minutes. There are different brands on the market. A gallon will go a long way. Directions for proper mixing are printed on the container labels. Any dealer in boat supplies will gladly give you all the necessary information about the resin he carries.

Another product which can be used for experimenting in casting fishes comes in paste form and can be troweled directly into the mold; it is usually referred to as plastic paste.

I use a product called "Hysol" which is produced by Houghton Laboratories Inc., Olean, New York. It is packaged in liquid form and when mixed is self-setting; no heating is required to set it. For casting all types of fishes, I have found it extremely satisfactory. When mixed with some whiting or asbestos, it forms a composition that is hard and yet easy to work with a tool.

I usually order a gallon of Hysol–ERL 2795 and a quart of Hysol–ERL 2793. The material is mixed four parts 2795 to one part 2793. In this state it is rather thin, very fluid, and will flow down to the bottom of the mold. In other words, when troweling the substance, it will not stay in quantity on inclined surfaces unless it is mixed with whiting or asbestos. I suggest that the first coat in molding a fish contain mostly whiting as a filler in the Hysol. A small portion of asbestos added to the mixture will help prevent excessive flowing (formula No. 1). Too much asbestos in the first layer will produce pin holes or air holes in the cast. The second or reinforcing layer can include a greater proportion of asbestos (formula No. 2).

For a medium size fish, I find it convenient to use these amounts: four jiggers of 2975 to one jigger of 2793. With the whiting and asbestos added there is enough material to work easily before it begins to set. Scrape the bowl clean with a spatula or dull knife as soon as possible and then clean it with a piece of cheesecloth and about a jigger of commercial alcohol.

The Hysol always has to be mixed four to one. However, as far as the addition of whiting and asbestos is concerned, the individual can vary the amounts one way or the other to arrive at a consistency which may be more suitable to his needs.

Formalin

Formalin is a colorless liquid which has a pungent odor and vapors which are intensely irritating to mucous membranes. It is a preservative and a disinfectant. Formalin is a saturated aqueous solution of formaldehyde gas in water, about 37 per cent formaldehyde by weight.

A 10 per cent solution is usual for preserving fishes: nine parts water to one part Formalin. An 8 per cent solution may be used for large fishes, and a less potent solution of 15 per cent may be used for small specimens.

Formalin may be purchased in most chemical supply shops and is inexpensive. It usually is contained in a fairly rugged bottle. However, great care should be taken so that the bottle will not break during transit. A full strength solution of Formalin spilled on the floor of a car will force its occupants to leave. The only way to relieve the situation is to douse the area repeatedly with water, and then with formula No. 3. Then, the area may be doused again with water.

Formalin should always be treated with respect. If splashed into the eyes by accident, permanent impairment of vision may occur unless the eyes are bathed with fresh water quickly and repeatedly.

Rubber gloves should be worn if Formalin specimens are to be handled for any length of time. If a specimen is to be changed from one container to another, a rinse of the hands in water will suffice.

Glue a label marked POISON prominently on the receptacle; and, of course, keep it under lock and key where children cannot touch it. If jars with fishes preserved in Formalin are displayed, children should not touch them without supervision. It is imperative that the jars be so placed that no one can knock them off the shelf accidentally.

When transporting Formalin, I pack the jars in a strong wooden box which has a hinged top and a provision for a padlock. If the Formalin is shipped, I screw the top down as an added precaution. The box is divided into wooden compartments, each wide enough to hold a "Ball jar" of Formalin with excelsior packing around it—including the bottom. Before the top is closed, pack more excelsior in a layer which will cover all the tops of the jars. Include enough packing so that when the cover of the box comes down, there is absolutely no indication of jar movement within. I have sent Formalin in this manner to such distant places as India and back again with jars full of specimens, without breaking.

Formalin is a wonderful preservative. Its use certainly should not be curtailed because it is a poison. This chemical is perfectly safe if common sense and caution are exercised while handling it.

Sterine

Sterine is a greasy, liquid substance that is excellent as a separator in preventing freshly mixed plaster from adhering to plaster which has set, as in a two-piece mold. It is also used on table tops when working with plaster. Plaster is easily scraped from an area that has been covered with sterine. The solution is prepared by mixing steric acid and kerosene. Simply place some powdered steric acid in a jar and add kerosene until it is well mixed into a smooth consistency. The sterine should not be so thick as to be lumpy. It is best applied with a brush. Keep it in a closed jar when stored. Sterine thickens in a cool room; warm it near a radiator and the consistency will thin.

Steric acid is a product derived from the fat of beef cattle. It is obtainable in powdered form or block form. If available only in the latter condition, it has to be scraped into a receptacle of kerosene by using a bent hack-saw blade. Chemical supply houses carry steric acid at about a dollar and a half per pound. A pound is sufficient to make a mixture for many molds.

Alum

Alum is an astringent mineral. It is mixed with water and used (in this instance) to facilitate the setting of plaster of Paris over the fluids and slime that may remain on a fish's body after cleaning the specimen in preparation for molding. It is available at any drug store. A handful in a small pan of water is enough to treat both sides of a medium size fish.

Glycerin

Glycerin, also known as glycerol, is a sweet, oily, nearly colorless liquid obtainable at drug stores or chemical supply houses. It is viscous and is often added to glue and other materials to make them less brittle.

Asbestos

Asbestos, dextrine, and whiting are the main ingredients in mixing a batch of casting compound.

Asbestos, also called earth-flax or mountain-cork, is a white or gray mineral and has wide use in fire- and acid-resisting articles. Plumbers and furnace men use it to insulate pipes. For fish preparation, ground gray asbestos is best. It is an inexpensive material and usually comes in 50-pound bags.

Dextrin

Dextrin is a carbohydrate found in nature in the sap of plants. It has adhesive qualities and is soluble in water; it is often used as a substitute for gum arabic. It also comes in large bags and is inexpensive.

Whiting

Whiting is a finely powdered washed chalk which is used as a pigment and for polishing. It also makes a fine "filler" in many substances; it is inexpensive.

FORMULAS

1. Synthetic Casting Material
   Hysol—obtained from Houghton Laboratories, Olean, New York.

   ERL 2795—4 parts
   ERL 2793—1 part
   Whiting—1½ to 2½ cups

   A jigger or two of asbestos will prevent flowing of the mixture in the mold.

2. Synthetic Casting Material
    Hysol

    ERL 2795—4 parts
    ERL 2793—1 part
    Whiting—2 cups
    Asbestos—½ to 1 cup

3. Formalin Odor Dispenser
    1260 grams sodium bisulfite
    840 grams sodium sulfite
    5 gallons tap water

    Dunk Formalin specimens in this solution for a few minutes.
    (There are 454 grams in a pound.)

4. Wax—For Brushing into Molds
    "Parawax" or paraffin—5 ounces
    Rosin (colophony)—8 ounces
    Carnauba wax—1 ounce

5. Wax—For Pouring into Molds
    "Parawax" or paraffin—8 ounces
    Carnauba wax—2 ounces
    Rosin—2 ounces
    Turpentine or benzine—1½ drams

6. Separator in Casting
    Vaseline—⅓
    Beeswax or petroleum wax—⅔

    Shave wax into a jar of kerosene; let stay overnight; add the
    Vaseline. Should be consistency of cold cream. Strain through
    cheesecloth if necessary. When the shellac in the mold has
    dried, apply the separator with your fingers. Rub it into every
    detail. The separator will spread smoothly with the warmth
    of your hand. Be sure to work it in well, and do not apply an
    excessive amount—wipe away until a thin but effective coat
    covers every bit of area.

7. Glue—Glycerin Solution
   Glue—9 parts
   Glycerin—1 part

   Warm glue in double boiler; when thin, add glycerin and mix thoroughly. Always warm glue for thinning and stir before applying.

8. Casting Compound
   Dextrin—5 pounds
   Whiting—5 pounds
   Asbestos—5 pounds
   Water—1 gallon
   Glycerin—3 ounces
   Carbolic acid—1 teaspoon

   Mix whiting and asbestos in a large receptacle which has room to spare. Boil the water and add dextrin gradually. Keep stirring or the dextrin will settle to the bottom in chunks. Add glycerin and carbolic acid to dextrin and water. Pour the solution into the basin or bucket which holds the asbestos and whiting. Mix thoroughly.

   This mixture can be stored in an air-tight container for an indefinite period of time. I usually prepare a batch that will fill a 10-gallon crock, and then I remove the compound by the panful whenever necessary.

   When ready for casting, add water and mix well until the mixture is well thinned out. Then keep adding plaster of Paris and kneading the compound until it reaches a heavy consistency which can be spread easily with a spatula.

Index

Alum, 25, 208
Asbestos, 17, 25–27, 37

Belly contours, 10, 11, 25
Big-game fishes
　mold, 198
　preparing, 198
Bills, 78, 80
　letter openers from, 156
　marlin, 148–51
　preparation of, 152, 153
　preserving, 148, 151
　sailfish, 148, 149, 151
　sawfish, 148, 150
　swordfish, 148, 149
　trophies, as, 148

Cameras, 3, 4
Cast
　color in, 47
　fins, plastic, 39
　glass eye in, 48
　head, 147, 148
　medallion-type, 45
　mold, preparing for, 38, 41
　painting, ready for, 39, 40
　plaque, 45
　plaster, 14, 38, 45–47
　plastic, 41, 46, 59, 60–63, 66
　　cleaning, 70–74
　　finishing, 70, 74
　　open mouth, 71
　　removing from mold, 70
　　seams in, 72
　resin, 59, 66
　shellac on, 48
　show side of, 49
　wax, 38, 48–54
　　painting, 53, 54

Casting compound, 38, 41, 55–58, 197
cast
　defects, 58
　drying, 58
　repairs, 58
　formula, 211
Celluloid fins, 47, 55
Collecting
　field, in the, 161–63
　foreign countries, in, 190
　rod and reel, by, 161
　seining, by, 161–64
　trapping, by, 164, 165
Color
　casts, in, 47
　combinations, silhouettes, 121, 122
　fish mounts, 188
　fishes, of, 4
　markings, fresh fish, 7
　molds, in, 47
　notes, 3, 7, 16
　photographs, 3, 5
　schemes, 123, 124
　silhouettes, 122
　spectrum, 122, 123
　transparencies, 3
　wax, in, 51, 53
　wheel, 122, 124
Conduit pipe
　cast reinforcement, 66, 67
　material, 204
　mold reinforcement, 33, 66, 176, 179, 194, 195
Crating, field, 181, 182
Customs, 190, 191

Dextrin, definition of, 209
Dry ice, 7, 8
Drying, mold, 23, 31

213

Eye, criteria, 187

Field
  collecting, 161–63
  crating, 181, 182, 195
  fins, care of, 196–98
  laboratory, 193
  molding, 31, 32, 35, 175–81, 194–96
  notes, 4
  observation, 199
  preparation, 193
  seining, 161
  sketches, 4
  skinning, 12
  specimens
    care of, 3, 199
    preserving, 8, 168
    protecting, 4
    wrapping, 4
  work, professional, 172, 174–77, 188, 189, 192
Fins
  anchoring, 55
  artificial, 55, 58
  base, 30
  carved, 56
  cast, 56
  Celluloid, 47, 52, 55
  criteria, 187
  curvatures of, 187
  field, in the, 196–98
  mold, 74
    areas in, 43–45
  molding, 27–29
    preparations before, 16, 25
  mounts, repairs on, 200, 201
  originals, drying, 100
  painting, 109
  plaster, 47
  plastic, 55, 73–77
    cutting, 71
  position of, 187
  wax, 52, 53, 55
Formalin
  definition of, 206
  jars, display, 169, 170
  neutralizer, 168
  odor dispenser, 81, 168, 207, 210
  packing, 8
  receptacles, 10, 11, 169, 170, 192
  shipping, 8, 10
  solutions, 10, 206, 207

  specimens
    care of, 207
    display, 160, 168, 170
    packing, 193
    permanent storage of, 168
    preparation of, 166, 167
    preserving in, 165, 166
Formulas, 203, 209–11
  casting compound, 211
  Formalin odor dispenser, 210
  glue-glycerin, 211
  separator in casting, 210
  synthetic casting material (plastic or resin), 209, 210
  wax
    brushing into mold, 210
    pouring into mold, 210
Freezing, frozen specimens, 6–8, 12, 13, 35

Glass eye
  in cast, 48
  painting, 78, 115
  setting into plastic cast, 74
Glycerin
  definition of, 208
  glue, formula, 211

Heads
  cast, 147, 148
  preserved, 142–45
  mold, 147
  mounted, 146–48
  mounts, repair on, 201, 202
Hypodermic syringe, 10

Keys (V-shaped), mold, shelf of, 17, 19, 26, 27, 29

Lacquer
  painting, 113–15
  preserved heads, 145
  separator, 25, 26
Letter opener
  bills
    marlin, 156
    sailfish, 156
  preparation, 157, 158

Markings
  notes on, 7
  photos for, 9

Materials, 203–8
  alum, 208
  asbestos, 209
  casting compound, 209
  conduit pipe, 204
  dextrin, 209
  Formalin, 206
  glycerin, 208
  plaster, 204
  plastic, 205, 209
  resin, 205
  sisal, 204
  steric acid, 208
  sterine, 208
  synthetic casting, 209
  whiting, 208
  woven glass, 204
Mold
  big-game fishes, 198
  chisel chipping of, 47
  color in, 47
  crating, 181, 182, 195
  drying, 23
  edges, cleaning, 34
  field, in the, 179–82, 196
  fins, areas of, 43–45
  fish, removing from, 31, 179, 180
    setting in plaster, 195
  four-piece, 15, 175
  half
    pouring plaster, 95
    rear, 41
    skin mount, 93–95, 97–99
    wax cast, 49
  halves
    securing, 69
    separating, 22, 27, 31, 64, 65
    wiring, 31, 34
  head, 147
  keys, 17, 19, 26, 27, 29
  mouth, open, 24, 26, 78
  one-piece, 194
  plaster, 14, 17, 19, 25
  plaster casts, 46
  plastic cast, removal, 70
  preparing for cast, 38, 41
  rear side, cutting, 23
  receptacles for, 36
  reinforcing, 22, 29, 33, 35, 176, 179,
    194, 195
  repairing, 38
  shelf, 17, 19, 21, 31
  shelves, cleaning, 41

  shipping, 191
  show side, 34, 41
  two-piece, 15, 30, 31, 33, 41, 49, 54,
    194
  wall side, 45
  wax, for, 49
Molding
  field, in the, 31, 32, 35, 175–80,
    182, 194
  fins, 27–29
  home, 31, 35–37
  laboratory, 31, 36, 37
  plaster, 14, 15, 18, 21
    per fish, 193
    per type of fish, 193
  preparations before, 16–17
  receptacles for, 36
  skin, filling before, 35, 36
  tracing fish before, 36
Mounts
  body curvatures, 186
  color, 188
  criteria, 188
  eye, 186–88
  fin, 186
  head, 146, 147
  mouth, 186
  museum, 190
  old specimen, 190
  painting, 188
  repairing, 200–202
  skin, 81
Mouth
  criteria, 187
  mold, 24, 26, 78
  open, 10
  plastic cast of, 71, 79
Museums
  amateur, 159, 161
  exhibits, amateur, 170, 171
  field work, 188, 189
  fish mounts, 185
  history, 183–85
  methods, 31
  natural history, 172

Notes
  color of fishes, 3, 7, 16
  field, 4
  markings on fishes, 7

Outlines
  burnt in wood, 125–28

Outlines (*continued*)
  drawing, 12
  pen and ink, 118
  trophy fish, 116, 117

Painting
  airbrush, 113, 114
  chrome base, 108
  fine markings, 108
  fins, 109
  glass eye, 78, 115
  lacquer, 113, 114
  methods, simple, 112
  mount, 104–8, 188
    wall side of, 110
  oils and brush, 112, 113
  pearl essence, 108
  preparing surface before, 104–6
  varnish, 110
  wax cast, 53, 54
Photographs
  arrangement of, 141
  before molding fish, 16
  color, 3, 5, 9
  composition of, 133–40
  hints, 133, 140, 141
  mounting of, 141
  reference, modeling skin, 36
  trophies, as, 133–41
Plaster
  amount per fish, 193
  applying, 26
  casts, 14, 38, 45
  fins, 47
  for molding, 193
  keys, 27
  material, 204
  mixing, 15, 193
  mold, 14, 18, 21, 25
  packing for shipment, 192
  price, 14
  receptacles, 27, 36, 192, 193
  setting, 27
  shelf, 27
  shipment, 192, 193
  splash coat, 26
Plastic
  applying, 59, 61
  asbestos mix, 63
  casting, 60, 62
  casts, 41, 59, 60, 62, 63, 66, 67
  fins, 55, 73–77

formulas, 209, 210
materials, 205, 206
mouth, 78, 79
reinforcement, 62, 66–69
removal from mold, 63
Powder
  copper, 51
  glass, 51
  gold, 51
  marble meal, 51
  silver, 51
Preservatives
  arsenic, 89
  Formalin, 89
  salt, 89
  skin, for, 89

Receptacles
  Formalin, 10, 11, 169, 170, 192
  molding, for, 36
  plaster, 27, 192
  salt, 13
Reinforcing
  cast
    plaster, 46
    plastic, 63, 66, 67
  conduit pipe, with, 33, 66, 67, 176, 179, 194, 195
  mold, 22, 29, 33, 35, 176, 179, 194, 195
  sisal, with, 19, 22
  wax, 52
  woven glass, with, 63, 66, 67
Repairing
  body of mount, 200, 201
  fins, 200, 201
  head of mount, 200, 201
  mold, 38
  skin of body, 200, 201
Resin
  cast, 59, 66
  casting formulas, 209, 210
  material, 205, 206
  wax, in, 50

Separator
  formula, 210
  lacquer, 26
  soap, 49, 52
  sterine, 21, 24
  Vaseline, 27
  wax-plaster, 49

Shark jaws
    preparation of, 156
    trophies, as, 153–55
Shelf
    around fish, 17, 25
    asbestos, 17, 25–27, 37
    keys, 17, 19, 26
    mold, 19, 21
    plaster, 27
    sand, 17, 25, 27
    soil, 17, 25
Shellac
    bill base, 152
    burnt wood outlines, 128
    casting compound, 59
    mold, 41, 45, 56
    painting, 104, 106
    plaster cast, 48
    shark jaws, 156
    skin mount, 202
    stain, 132
    wax, 54
    wood mannequin, 92
Shipping
    foreign, 190, 191
    Formalin, 8, 10, 192
    materials, 190–92
    plaster, 192
Silhouettes, 116–23
    art board, 118
    color, 121–23
        combinations, 121
    trophies, as, 5
    wood, 128–32
Sisal
    cast, plaster reinforcement, 46
    material, 204
    mold
        reinforcement, 19, 22
        repair, 38
Skin
    cleaning, 88
    filling before molding, 35
    freezing, 13
    preserving, 12, 88, 89
    salting, 13
Skin mounts, 81
    backboard, 99, 101
    casting compound, 101
    excelsior body, 91
    full mold, 101–3
    half mold, 93–99
    one side, 90

    reinforced, 98
    removed from mold, 99
    repair of, 200
    wood mannequin, 91, 92
Skinning, 6, 12, 81–88
Slime removal, 15, 25, 26
Soap separator, 49, 52
Spears
    letter openers, as, 156
    marlin, 148–51
    mold of, 78
    preparation of, 152, 153
    preserving, 148, 151
    sailfish, 148, 151
    sawfish, 148, 151
    swordfish, 148, 149
    trophies, as, 148
Specimens
    collecting, 4
    display in Formalin, 160, 161, 168–
        70
    field care of, 199
    Formalin, 81
    freezing, 6, 8
    frozen, 12, 35
    preparing for Formalin, 166, 167
    preparing for molding, 15, 25
    preserved, 11, 12, 165
    protecting, 4, 6
    removing from mold, 179
    salting skin of, 6
    show side of, 6, 25
    shrinkage of, 11
    spoilage of, 0, 11
    storage of, in Formalin, 168
Spoilage, prevention of, 6, 11
Steric acid, definition of, 208
Sterine
    definition of, 208
    preparing, 208
    separator, 21, 24, 208

Tails
    preserved, 145, 146
    trophies, as, 145, 146
Trap, collecting by, 164, 165
Trophies
    bills, 148, 156
    heads, 142–46
    letter openers, 156, 158
    photographs, 133–41
    shark jaws, 153–55
    silhouettes, 5, 116–23, 128–32

Trophies (*continued*)
  spears, 148
  special, 142
  tails, 145, 146

Vaseline
  separator, 27
    formula, 210
Vinegar, 25

Wax
  bending, 54
  brushing into mold, 51–53
  carnauba, 50
  cast, 8, 49–54
  cementing, 54
  colophony, 50
  color, 51, 53
  defects, 53
  fillers, 51
  finishing, 54
  fins, 52, 53, 55

formulas, 210
painting, 53, 54
pouring into mold, 51, 52
reinforcement, 52
removal from mold, 53
repairs, 53
resin, 50
rosin, 50
seams, 54
separator, 52
trimming, 54
whiting, 51
Whiting
  definition of, 208
  wax, in, 51
Wire hangers
  plaster cast, 46, 48
  wax cast, 52
Wiring mold, 31, 34, 69
Woven glass
  material, 204
  plastic cast reinforcing, 63, 66, 67